The No-Nonsense
Guide to
Project Management

The No-Nonsense Guide to Project Management

Barbara Allan

facet
publishing

© Barbara Allan 2017

Published by Facet Publishing
7 Ridgmount Street, London WC1E 7AE
www.facetpublishing.co.uk

Facet Publishing is wholly owned by CILIP:
the Library and Information Association.

British Library Cataloguing in Publication Data
A catalogue record for this book is available from the British Library.

ISBN 978-1-78330-203-1 (paperback)
ISBN 978-1-78330-204-8 (hardback)
ISBN 978-1-78330-205-5 (e-book)

First published 2017

Text printed on FSC accredited material.

Typeset from author's files in 11/14pt Revival 565 and Frutiger by Flagholme Publishing Services.
Printed and made in Great Britain by CPI Group (UK) Ltd, Croydon, CR0 4YY.

Contents

List of tables and figures

Tables

Figures

List of case studies

Acknowledgements

I would like to thank all the library and information workers who have had an input to this book. This may have been through their participation in my workshops delivered at the Chartered Institute of Library and Information Professionals (CILIP) and other organisations, or through their publications, websites and blogs, or in informal discussions. Special thanks to Ann Munn and Fiona O'Brien of the University of Westminster, Juanita Foster-Jones, CILIP, and Lisa Jeskins, an independent trainer, who provided me with detailed case studies on their current experiences of project management. Thank you to everyone who was involved in the Learning Futures programme at the University of Westminster between 2012 and 2015, and in particular to the professional project management team who provided inspiration for some of the ideas and examples of project management practices which are contained in this book.

An earlier book of mine, *Project Management: Tools and Techniques for Today's ILS Professional* (Facet Publishing, 2004) informed this one. A number of my personal examples are repeated in this book as I was unable to find suitable examples which made the same point. Writing this book has been an interesting learning experience as there has been a shift in the use of information and communications technology (ICT) to support project management. There are now many examples of project management software available to library and information workers, and social media has transformed the communications process. Crowdfunding and crowdsourcing are now important sources of resources (funding, volunteers, archives), which are used to develop and maintain some projects. This book attempts to capture the current situation in project management in libraries and information services, and I imagine that it will continue to change and develop, particularly in response to developments in ICT and their applications.

Finally, thank you to Denis and Sarah, who have been patient and supportive during my time working on this book.

Barbara Allan

Introduction to the book

Introduction to the chapter

This chapter introduces the concept of project management and its application in library and information services, and it considers the following topics:

- different types of projects
- project work and the library and information profession
- professional development in project management
- how to work as an effective project manager or team member.

This is followed by an overview of the structure and contents in this book, *No-Nonsense Guide to Project Management*.

About this book

This book provides a practical guide to project management in the context of library and information work. Project work is widespread across the sector and colleagues may work on relatively small-scale local projects, such as introducing family history workshops within a public library service, or large complex projects, such as developing shared services across a number of libraries. Small-scale and simple projects may be led by an individual who works on the project by themselves or with a small team. In contrast, complex or large-scale projects may involve people from different professions and organisations, and they may be managed by a team of professional project managers.

This book introduces a wide range of tools and techniques used in project management within library and information services, and gives examples and case studies taken from a variety of projects from many different kinds of library and information services in the UK and across the world. Readers may use this book to gain an understanding of different approaches to project management and their suitability for different types of projects. The book also considers the people side of projects, including how to manage change (essential for strategic projects) and how to work in partnership.

Introduction to project management

What is a project? A simple definition of a project is that it is an activity that:

- has a clear aim and set of outcomes
- involves innovation and change
- has limited resources, e.g. staff time, budget
- has an agreed start and end date.

These are some examples of common projects within library and information services:

- moving a library
- introducing a new service
- developing shared services
- digitising a collection
- merging two libraries
- introducing a new performance management system
- introducing new employment contracts
- building and moving into a new learning resource centre
- producing a new staff development programme
- introducing a new ICT system or service
- re-branding a library and its services
- developing a blended learning course.

Figure 1.1 on the next page provides a series of questions to help you decide whether or not you are working on a project.

Project management is the approach an organisation, team or individual take to ensure that the project achieves its aim and objectives, and that it is delivered on time and within budget. There are several approaches to project management, depending on the size and complexity of the project. Small-scale or simple projects which are led by a sole library or

Project characteristics	Your responses
1. Is there a clear aim and set of outcomes (these may be formally written down or have been agreed informally)?	
2. Does the activity involve introducing something new, e.g. a service, or product, to the library and information service?	
3. Does the activity involve change, e.g. to current working practices?	
4. Are you working with limited resources, e.g. staff time, a budget?	
5. Is there an agreed start date?	
6. Is there an agreed end date?	
If you answer three or more questions with a 'yes' then you are working on a project and it is advisable to use the project management tools and techniques outlined in this book. Even if you answer 'yes' to a few of these questions then project management tools and techniques may help you to be successful in this work.	

Figure 1.1 *Is it a project?*

information worker may be project managed using very simple tools and techniques, and organised with the help of a diary and spreadsheet. In contrast, large-scale or complex projects normally use standard project management methodologies, such as PRINCE2®, use standard processes and techniques, and may require a specialist team of project managers and support workers. Project management methodologies are explored in Chapter 2. These different approaches to project management are considered throughout the book and, where possible, case studies are provided to illustrate current practices.

Different types of projects

There are many different types of projects, which may be classified using the following headings:

- strategic or operational projects
- simple or complex projects
- local or distributed projects.

Strategic or operational projects
Strategic projects (or programmes) are those that involve a major change

within the library or information service, for example a change in direction (strategy), which may be linked to a new vision and mission, and related goals and outcomes. This might lead to a change in the culture and identity of the library and information service. Strategic change often takes years to achieve and it is likely to include project management and management of change tools and techniques. Examples of strategic change include the merger of two distinct library services, the introduction of new policies and practices relating to customer services. Typically, senior members of the library and information service provide project leadership and management.

Library and information workers may work on strategic change projects or programmes led by their institution, for example, the introduction of a new performance management system; the introduction of new employment contracts with associated working conditions and practices; the introduction of shared services; or developing a new library and information service in another location, e.g. overseas. In these types of projects, the director of the library and information service is likely to be a member of the strategic board or steering group for the change process and individual members of the library service work in different teams or task groups on the project.

In contrast, operational projects are less likely to involve major changes and may be located within a particular team or department. The project manager may be a team leader or individual member of the team. Their time frame may be relatively short, e.g. six months, and they are unlikely to involve the significant use of management of change tools and techniques.

It is important to recognise that operational projects require the development and implementation of a communications strategy. Examples of operational projects include organising a conference, developing a new service, digitising a collection and developing a new course or workshop.

If you lead a project it is worth considering the level of the project: is it a strategic or operational project? This is important as strategic projects require a more detailed management of change process than operational projects. Project managers who are not aware of this difference may find that although the technical aspects of a strategic project are successful the project as a whole fails or falters as insufficient attention has been paid to the people side of the change. Management of change is considered in Chapter 9 and more detailed information and advice is available from Coleman and Thomas (2017); Hodges (2016); Phillips, Phillips and Weber (2016); or Pugh (2017).

Simple or complex projects

At the very start of any project, it is important to analyse its level of complexity. Projects range from relatively simple ones, e.g. developing a new workshop, through to extremely complex ones, e.g. an international project involving six different libraries and technical innovations. The more complex the project the more likely it is to succeed if you use formal project management tools and techniques. In contrast, simple projects may be developed and delivered using basic project management tools and ideas. Table 1.1 on the next page illustrates some of the factors that need to be taken into account when working out whether or not you are starting a simple or complex project. It is worth noting that some small-scale projects may be extremely complex and large-scale projects may be simple.

Local or distributed projects

Another important factor in analysing a project is to think about its geography. Many projects are located within a library and information service in one building, which makes it much easier for the staff working on the project to communicate with each other either formally or informally, and face-to-face communications are relatively easy. In contrast, other projects involve people working across different buildings, cities or countries. International projects may include people working across different time zones and they may have a variety of first languages, so some people are not working in their native language. They are also less likely to have face-to-face communications except through online tools such as Skype or FaceTime. Clearly, a project where everyone is co-located in the same building is likely to be simpler to manage than an internationally distributed one.

Project work and the library and information profession

Library and information workers may be involved in project work in various ways: leading and managing a project within their own service; leading or participating in a project that works with several organisations, e.g. a collaborative digitisation project; or participating in a project that is led by another part of their organisation. Therefore project workers may work within the library and information profession either within their own library or across a number of libraries, e.g. if they are working on an international digitisation project, or work in multi-professional teams either within their own institution or across organisations.

Table 1.1 *Comparison of the characteristics of simple and complex projects*

Characteristics	Simple projects	Complex projects
Boundaries	Clearly identified and relatively straightforward	Complex, difficult to define and involve many interfaces
Data	Relatively low volumes	Large volumes
Environment	Well known to project worker(s); relatively little change during lifetime of project	Turbulent; external factors, e.g. changes in government policy or the exchange rate, may have impact on project
Innovation	Low levels; although the project may be novel for the project team, there is existing experience and good practice in this area of work within the sector	High levels
Leadership and management	Project manager has complete leadership and management control over project	Provided by steering group or board, which approves any strategic changes to the project; project management is shared among several individuals
People	Individual or small team working within the same department or library service	Project involves many activities carried out by people from different professional backgrounds, teams or organisations; different cultures and countries, with a range of first languages; and living and working in different time zones
Risks	Easily identified and manageable	Hard to identify; some may be difficult to manage and beyond the control of the project team and board
Technology	Relatively well established and tested	New and relatively untested
Working methods	Tried and tested (even if they are new to the project team)	New to the project team and may not have been developed elsewhere, consequently may be invented as part of the project

Library and information workers at different stages in their careers need to be aware of their own responsibilities and the level(s) at which they are working or contributing to the project. There are three types of roles involved in a project – leader, project manager and project worker – and these are outlined below.

Leader
The leader is responsible for:

- establishing the strategy
- making strategic decisions
- ensuring the availability of sufficient resources
- dealing with major issues
- communicating with key stakeholders
- working with the project manager.

Project manager
The project manager is responsible for:

- working with the project leader and project team
- gaining formal approval for the project
- developing a project plan
- implementing the plan
- managing people and resources
- monitoring the project
- communicating with stakeholders
- evaluating the project
- disseminating information about the project and its outcomes.

Project worker
The project worker is responsible for:

- working with the project manager and team
- successfully completing project tasks
- working in a team
- communicating with project manager and other colleagues.

The number of people involved in a project depends on its size and complexity. Table 1.2 compares the roles of people working on simple or small-scale and complex or large-scale projects.

Table 1.2 *The roles of the different people working on a project*

Type of project	Roles	People involved with the project
Simple	Leader Manager Team worker	One librarian
Complex	Leader Manager Team worker	Librarian leads project 3 project managers each lead a different aspect of the project Each project manager works with a team of 3 project workers
Very complex or large-scale and simple	Leader Manager Team worker	Director of company or host organisation leads project; librarian is a member of the project board 10 project managers each lead a different aspect of the project Each project manager works with a team of 3–10 project workers

Many library and information workers manage simple projects where they take on the roles of leader, project manager and project worker, possibly in addition to their normal roles. Clearly, this can be very challenging and the use of basic project management tools and techniques may be very helpful in making the project process clear and explicit. The tools are beneficial as they use tried and tested methods to communicate the progress of the project (and any issues) to managers and stakeholders.

In the past decade, there has been an increase in the number of project management professionals who work with library and information workers on major projects. Typically, project management professionals are likely to have an undergraduate or postgraduate degree in project management plus formal practical qualifications, for example in PRINCE2®. Some organisations employ a team of professional project managers who work on specific projects as determined by the organisation's objectives and resources. Alternatively, professional project managers may be recruited on short-term contracts to manage the project. In the example provided in Table 1.2, each of the three project managers may be professional project managers rather than a library or information worker. If project managers come from a specialist team within the institution they will understand its culture although they may not be familiar with the working practices in the library and information service. If external project managers are recruited they may have experience of working in a particular sector, such as health or academic libraries. In contrast, some external project managers may have little or no experience of the sector and require time to understand the culture of the service and the detail of the systems and processes.

Professional development in project management

Project management is regularly considered to be either a core or an enabling competency for library and information professionals. For example, it is included in CILIP's model of Professional Knowledge Skills and Behaviours (PKSB) under the generic skills of strategy, planning and management (see CILIP.org.uk):

> 10.9 Project management
> Understanding and applying a set of principles and tools for defining,
> planning, managing and completing a time limited business task (project),
> within agreed parameters of costs and resources, timescales and quality.

The US Special Libraries Association (see www.sla.org) and the Canadian Association of Research Libraries (see www.car-abrc.ca) identify project management as a competence.

Schwartz's (2016) survey of directors of academic and public libraries identified project management as one of the 11 skills that are essential for librarians. This raises the issue of whether or not project management should have a major place within the curriculum of library and information studies as it is frequently located within a module such as managing library and information services.

Increasingly, many library and information professionals are adding project management tools and techniques to their portfolio. This topic is explored by Horwath (2012), with reference to project management in Canadian libraries, and she listed the following approaches to development:

- a college or university providing a formal course
- holding seminars, webinar, conference presentations
- reading books or articles
- reading websites or blogs
- an employer providing in-house training.

This list is similar to the one I developed through informal conversations with library and information workers in academic, public and special libraries in the UK, as well as independent consultants and trainers. In the past two years, I have noticed that a number of colleagues are now using professional short courses, e.g. in PRINCE2® or Agile, to enhance their knowledge, skills and CV. The results of Horwath's (2012) survey show that many librarians receive no training in this area and that reading is a major source of information and advice. The library and information workers Horwath surveyed agreed that they needed to develop project management skills, for the following reasons:

• Project work is common in all libraries and their strategic plans are often delivered using projects.
• As libraries become flatter organisations, there is a reduction in hierarchies and project work becomes more important.
• Projects are more cost-effective if they are managed efficiently.

Although project management may appear on the curriculum of programmes in library and information studies, it is rarely given much space, e.g. as indicated by a whole module on the topic, and the current evidence suggests that new graduates in the profession would benefit from developing a range of professional project management tools and techniques.

Case study 1.1   Developing knowledge and skills in project management

Nihal is a chartered librarian with a postgraduate qualification in library and information science. She works as a liaison librarian in an academic library in the UK. Following her involvement in a digitisation programme, she realised that she thoroughly enjoyed project work. She also noticed that there appeared to be many opportunities available to project workers. Nihal obtained her manager's permission to attend a one day course, 'The basics of project management', which the staff development department in her institution organised. She enjoyed the course but realised that it only scratched the surface of the topic. She decided to complete a more formal course in the subject and after researching what was available decided that she wanted to complete the PRINCE2® course and gain a formal qualification in project management. Nihal's manager said that her institution could not support her in taking this qualification. Although she was disappointed, Nihal decided to fund herself on the course and attended classes in her own time. She gained the PRINCE2® accreditation and used this to help her gain promotion within her own institution.

Working as an effective project manager or team member
This section provides general guidance on working as an effective project manager or team member. Individuals who are effective project managers and team workers are likely to pay attention to the following areas of their lives and these are outlined in the paragraphs below:

- looking after yourself and your well-being
- time management
- learning from experience
- gaining professional and career support
- using project work to support your career.

Looking after yourself
Key aspects of looking after yourself in the workplace include the following practices:

- Be organised. Use a diary and reminders. Keep a to-do list.
- Take part in training courses as these will help you to get to grips with the practices in your workplace.
- Know your work peaks and troughs. Most people have times of the day when they are full of energy and other times when their energy is low. For example some people are at their best in the morning (larks) while others are afternoon or evening people (owls). If you know your best times and you are able to organise when you carry out your work it makes sense to carry out your most demanding work when your energy levels are at their highest.
- Making sure that you take breaks. Eat healthy food. When you have a break, if possible get away from your desk and get some fresh air.
- Keep your working environment clean, tidy and uncluttered.
- Speak to your manager if you feel overwhelmed.
- Learn not to take on too much work.

Time management
Working on projects often requires very effective time management and problems may arise as a result of:

- poor initial project planning, particularly under-estimating the time requirements of the project work

- the project manager and team being over-ambitious and taking on a project that is not appropriately resourced
- growth of the project beyond its initial brief
- lack of a clear agreement between project workers and their managers about the division of time between running a library and information service and project work
- the staff being allocated too much work
- poor personal time management.

The use of the project planning techniques outlined in Chapters 3 and 4 should help prevent time management issues arising as a result of the first five issues listed. One special case is that of library and information workers who are involved in working on multiple projects who sometimes find that the demands of each project peak at the same time. If this coincides with a period of high demand from the library or information service it can be extremely stressful and the projects and library service could suffer as a result of the conflict. One important strategy to handle this situation is to manage the projects as a series of linked projects. Project management software, such as MS Project, provides tools that enable you to consolidate projects (see Chapter 7). Again, the issue may be avoided by detailed planning, including risk analysis.

Poor personal time management can be tackled through staff development, e.g. there are many courses available on this topic. Trelles-Duckett (2012) highlights five tips for project managers to manage time effectively:

- Stick to a framework.
- Focus on the plan.
- Be a good people manager.
- Keep your meetings on-topic and productive.
- Take time management seriously.

Table 1.3, opposite, lists some good habits in time management.

Learning from experience
The ability to reflect on and learn from our experiences is important to everyone as it forms the basis for personal learning, developing professional skills and organisational change. It offers a way of making the most of our experiences, e.g. of working on projects in different contexts, and it is a

Table 1.3 *Good habits of time management*

Topic	Good habits
Diary	Keep a diary and use electronic diary alerts
E-mails	Use e-mail flags to highlight key e-mails; use the folder facility; don't send unnecessary e-mails; keep e-mails as brief as possible
Online sources	Subscribe to essential online sources; unsubscribe from as many sources as possible
ICT	Invest time in learning how to use relevant ICT systems; attend relevant training sessions; make sensible decisions about whether or not to use ICT – many small projects can be managed effectively on paper
Information	Use existing sources; find out how much information is required; remember the Pareto effect: 20% of effort achieves 80% of the results
Interruptions	Switch off your phone and other interruptions, e.g. arrival of messages or e-mails; if possible find a quiet space to work, e.g. for report writing; let colleagues know that you cannot be interrupted as you are working to a deadline; if there is an interruption explain that you are working to a deadline and agree to meet later
Meetings	Always have an agenda; if necessary have timed agenda items and/or meetings
Paperwork	Keep paperwork as brief as possible; in meetings, record decisions and actions rather than whole discussions; use sticky notes to highlight action; use highlighter pens to mark out key pages or references
Prioritise	Prioritise work by organising it under the following headings: important and urgent, important but not urgent, urgent but not important, not important nor urgent; then deal with the tasks in the order listed and question whether those in the last category need to take place
Self-management	Be organised; take part in training courses; know your work peaks and troughs; take breaks; eat healthy food; when you have a break, if possible go away from your desk and get some fresh air; keep your working environment clean, tidy and uncluttered; speak to your manager if you feel overwhelmed; learn not to take on too much work
Self-reflection	Ask yourself regularly: what is the best use of my time right now?
Team working	Ask for and give support; help each other during peaks and troughs; discuss workloads; make time to celebrate your successes
Workloads	Set realistic deadlines; learn to say 'no'; use a daily and weekly 'to do' list; keep the project goals in mind

good way to remain alert and responsive in a changing environment. Reflection is the basis of self-awareness and can help distinguish previously unseen opportunities. Part of the reflective process is to identify an action that you will carry out: if reflection does not include an action-planning process it may become mere 'navel gazing'.

Reflection in the context of project management is an important process that involves the whole project team in thinking about and learning from their experiences. Individual project workers may want to keep a project learning diary to help them to capture their project experiences and learn from them. Project learning diaries are particularly useful for capturing many of the incidents or incidental events that are soon forgotten as the project progresses. These diaries may be kept as private and individual learning tools or as documents that can inform the final project reports. The project learning diary is meant to be a personal document: there is no right or wrong way to keep it.

One way of ensuring that reflection takes place is to decide on a regular time at which you will write your log and a fixed time each week to reflect back on it. It is not just writing in the log that is important, but the continuing reflection on what you have written. The following questions (which are not exhaustive) may suggest things you might write about as you keep your project learning diary. Use them in ways you wish or disregard them if you prefer to. They are only intended as a stimulus to help you focus on your experience and your reflection on it:

- Are things going to plan? If not, why not? What do I need to do differently?
- How do I feel about this project, process, task or activity? What am I enjoying? What do I dislike? What do I need to do differently?
- Select a critical incident. Briefly describe it. What contributed to this situation? What was my role in creating this situation? What do I need to do differently in future?

A quick method of maintaining a project learning diary is to keep notes daily or weekly, writing on one piece of paper divided into four sectors, as shown in Figure 1.2 on the next page. This structure is very similar to one presented in Chapter 6 on project evaluation.

Although the previous paragraphs relate to individual reflection using a project learning diary, the same processes may be applied to project teams.

Name:	Date:
What went well?	What could be improved?
What have I learnt?	What will I do as a result of this reflection?

Figure 1.2 *Sample structure of a project learning diary*

A simple way of encouraging project teams to reflect and learn from their experiences is to allocate some time to reflection at team meetings. E-mails or discussion groups may also be used to initiate and carry out reflective processes. The results of these activities can then be fed back into the project management activities and processes.

Gaining professional and career support
Professional and career support is important for all library and information professionals, including project managers, especially if you are new to project management, you are leading a large and complex project, or you are working as a solo professional on a project. There are many different sources of support, and mentoring – or learning by association with a role model – is a way of gaining support in:

- moving from one project to another
- dealing with a specific issue or problem
- developing skills for a particular task or project
- developing professional contacts and networks
- developing professionally.

There are many different sources of mentors and mentoring, including employers and professional bodies and networks. If you find that you do not have access to a mentor through one of these sources consider identifying your own mentor – most people are pleased to be able to support a colleague in this way.

As a project manager or worker it is well worth considering and possibly setting up a supportive mentoring process for yourself. Think about who may be able to act as your mentor and what you want to gain from the mentoring relationship. An information worker involved in two distinct projects may work with two mentors. The mentoring process involves meeting your mentor regularly, for example at three-monthly intervals, and exploring your current situation and career plan. If you are seeking someone to mentor you as you progress from one project to another, it is important to choose someone with experience of project work who keeps up to date with new ideas and professional developments. Someone who gives you time and space to explore your current issues and problems in confidence can be a vital source of support.

Using project work to support your career
Finally, projects are often a useful way of developing your knowledge and skills, gaining new professional experiences, and developing your network and contacts. They provide a channel through which you can develop your career and move towards your career goals. Project work may be used as a springboard to moving into management or leadership roles within library and information services, or in other sectors. Individuals who use project work successfully as a stepping stone are likely to identify the knowledge, skills and experience that they gained from their project work and use it to enhance their job application or curriculum vitae. Therefore it is worth looking out for opportunities to engage with appropriate projects that will help you to develop your knowledge and skills and enhance your career.

The structure of this book
Chapter 1 introduces the book and project management. It includes an exploration of different types of projects, e.g. small, simple, large and/or complex projects; a discussion about the library and information profession, and project work; and guidance on working as an effective project manager or team member.

Chapter 2 gives an overview of project management and introduces the three main themes that need to be taken into account when starting a project: project management tools and techniques, people and management of change. Three different approaches commonly used in library and information services are considered: the traditional approach, PRINCE2® and Agile. They are explained and advice in choosing the most appropriate approach for your project is given. This is followed by very brief sections that consider the people side of project management, and the management of change. These final two themes are followed up in much more detail in chapters 9 and 10.

Chapter 3 describes how to get started, outlining all the activities that need to take place before the project gains approval and can go ahead. Working through the ideas presented in this chapter can help ensure that you get off to a good start. At this early stage in the project process, you should start to think about defining the proposed project, the project leadership and management structures, and the people side of projects, including team work and communications. It is also important to think about technical aspects such as risk analysis, legal issues, finance and project documentation. The result of this work is a project brief – a short written summary of the proposed project, which is used to gain formal approval for it being approved.

Project planning is discussed in Chapter 4, which highlights the importance of undertaking detailed planning for successful project management, whether the project is small or large. Small projects require a project plan, which includes developing the project brief (see Chapter 3) and an action plan with an associated plan for the resourcing of the project (people and finances) as well as a risk analysis. This normally provides sufficient information to gain approval for the plan and for the project to go ahead. In contrast, large and complex projects require project management tools to produce a detailed schedule, which will help you to identify the workload of staff involved in the project. Specialist techniques such as Gantt charts and PERT diagrams are explained in this chapter. At this planning stage it is necessary to work out the detail of the project's documentation and communication processes and its finances, and provide an updated risk analysis. The detailed plan will then be pulled together as a report, which has to be approved by the project sponsor.

Once the project has been planned and approved the implementation process starts and this is considered in Chapter 5. During the implementation process, the project manager and team work on the project until it is complete. This chapter explores working with stakeholders, monitoring and reporting, identifying and managing problems and potential problems, communicating the project progress, reviewing the project process and project completion.

Chapter 6 is concerned with project evaluation and methods of disseminating the outcomes of the project. It outlines the factors that need to be taken into account when evaluating a project, including measuring its impact. Project evaluation provides an important means of learning from the experience. It is common practice to disseminate the outcomes of a project as a means for gaining publicity for the project, the library and information service, and the parent organisation. It also helps to share good practice and lessons learnt within the library and information profession. Dissemination of the outcomes of the evaluation process is considered in the second part of this chapter, which covers reports, community events, meetings, conference papers and presentations, and websites. It also highlights the value of social media in this communication process.

Chapter 7 explores the use of information and communications technologies (ICTs) to support project management. ICTs are used to help plan, organise and manage the project process, and to communicate to project team members and the wider group of stakeholders. This chapter discusses four types of ICT:

- everyday ICT tools, such as e-mail and spreadsheets, to help you to manage the project; this is all the technology required for many small or simple projects
- specialist purchased or free open source project management software used to manage projects; this is vital for large-scale and complex projects, particularly if they involve a large number of project workers
- collaborative tools that enable individuals and teams to communicate with each other and share documents, and provide online editing facilities; they may be used in all sizes of project
- social media and a range of commonly used tools from the perspective of project management.

Chapter 8 focuses on the money side of projects; although some library and information service projects are carried out within normal departmental budgets, many projects are funded from external sources, so many information workers become involved in obtaining external funding and managing a budget. The focus of this chapter is funding and obtaining funds from external sources, including through crowdfunding. The chapter covers current approaches to funding, external sources of funding, bidding and tendering for projects, crowdfunding, managing the finances, and audits.

Chapter 9 explores the people side of projects and the importance of managing relationships and communications throughout the project process. The topics covered in this chapter include fundamental requirements for project workers, developing working practices, working in diverse and virtual teams, and working with volunteers including when crowdsourcing.

Finally, Chapter 10 focuses on working in partnership on collaborative projects. It explores the following topics: the benefits of partnership working, the process of working in partnership and keeping the project together. The chapter ends with a series of case studies, which give a flavour of the realities of working in partnership.

References

Coleman, S. and Thomas, B. (2017) *Organisational Change Explained*, Kogan Page.

Hodges, J. (2016) *Managing and Leading People through Organisational Change*, Kogan Page.

Horwath, J. A. (2012) How Do We Manage? Project management in libraries, *Canadian Journal of Library and Information Practice and Research*, **7** (1), https://journal.lib.uoguelph.ca/.

Phillips, P., Phillips, J. and Weber, E. (2016) *Making Change Work*, Kogan Page.

Pugh, L. (2017) *Change Management in Information Services*, Routledge.

Schwartz, M. (2016) 'Top Skills for Tomorrow's Librarians; careers 2016', *Library Journal*, 9 March, http://lj.libraryjournal.com/2016/03/careers/top-skills-for-tomorrows-librarians-careers-2016/.

Trelles-Duckett, A. (2012) How to Manage your Time as a Project Manager, http://managementhelp.org/blogs/project-management/2012/06/01/how-to-manage-your-time-as-a-project-manager-by-andy-trainer/.

CHAPTER 2

An overview of project management

Introduction

This chapter provides an overview of project management to enable you to understand the different stages of the project management process and the importance of taking into account the people side of projects. Figure 2.1 illustrates the three main themes that need to be taken into account when starting a project: project management tools and techniques, people and the management of change. The main focus of this book is the first theme, project management tools and techniques. The people side of project work is considered in more detail in chapters 9 and 10.

In this chapter, three different approaches to project management are considered: the traditional approach, PRINCE2® and Agile. There is a

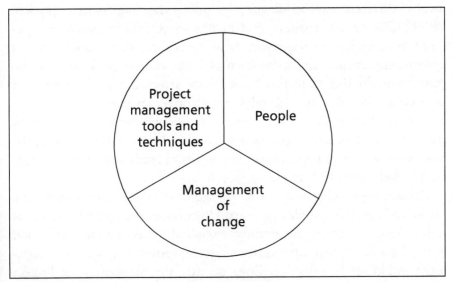

Figure 2.1 *Three themes of project management*

short explanation of the three approaches and advice on how to choose the most appropriate approach for your project. This is followed by sections that consider the people side of project management, and the management of change.

A brief history of project management

The concept of project management originated in large-scale military and industrial projects at a time when the so-called scientific approach to management dominated professional practices. As a result, project management developed from an assumption that the project leader operated in a traditional authoritarian manner and that a top-down approach was used to manage projects. This involved splitting the project into its constituent parts and then monitoring and controlling the project process.

Project management developed as a discipline in the 1950s and involved the use of techniques such as Gantt charts (which display project tasks and their time line), critical path methodology (a mathematical method of identifying critical tasks, which if carried out too late causes a delay in achieving the project's objectives), and programme review and evaluation technique (PERT), a mathematical method of displaying and calculating the times at which activities are carried out, developed as a result of large-scale projects. These techniques are described in Chapter 4.

There are many different approaches to project management, which involve different methodologies, including the traditional approach, PRINCE2®, critical chain project management, process-based management, lean project management, benefits realisation management and systems approaches. Exploring each of these approaches is likely to be counter-productive so in this book I have selected a small number of approaches according to their relevance to project management in library and information services. These are the traditional approach, PRINCE2® and Agile. Each of these approaches is outlined later in this chapter; the traditional approach should meet the needs of readers who are working on relatively small and simple projects.

Current approaches to project management evidence their historical origins in large and complex projects. However, in the current context of rapid change, political uncertainty, globalisation, economic booms and busts, the adherence to a top-down reductive approach to project management would not be effective. Consequently, the Association for Project Management (APM; https://www.apm.org.uk) states that project managers should approach their work in a flexible manner so that they can steer the project successfully through a changing environment (APM, 2016).

The APM suggest that, as well as standard project management tools and techniques, project managers need to develop the soft people skills of management and communication, as well as coaching and mentoring. The APM (2016) identify the important skills required by project managers as follows:

- Stakeholder management and communications
- Planning
- Budgeting/cost control and financial management
- Risk/issue management and opportunity management
- Decision making
- Leadership and line management
- Breadth/diversity of thinking
- Scheduling
- Resource management
- Quality management
- Strategic management
- Data and analytical skills and insight
- Coaching and mentoring
- Procurement
- Creativity.

The results of the APM (2016) survey demonstrate the importance of the people side of projects and it is now considered vital to the success of a project for project managers to identify all the different groups associated with their work and to develop and deliver an appropriate management and communications strategy. This involves people:

- working directly on the project, e.g. team workers and volunteers
- who are likely to be affected by the project, e.g. customers, co-workers and suppliers
- who have a stake in the library and information service and its success, e.g. board members or trustees, and senior managers in an organisation.

If the project is at a strategic level and involves a major change such as developing a shared service (see Chapter 1), it is likely to involve major cultural changes, so a 'management of change' process has to be developed and implemented at the same time as the project work takes place. This is considered briefly later in this chapter and then in more detail in Chapter 9. In addition, the need for staff development through training, coaching or mentoring may be required to ensure that project workers and colleagues have the necessary knowledge and skills to complete the project effectively, learn from the experience, and transfer this learning into their workplace for future work.

The traditional approach to project management

The traditional approach to project management is based on a project cycle of four stages: starting, planning, implementing and closing the project (Figure 2.2).

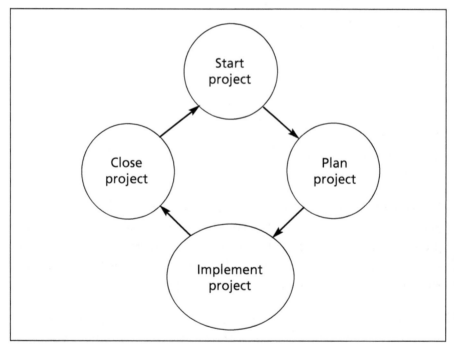

Figure 2.2 *The project life cycle*

In a simple project, starting involves:

• producing a project brief and justification

- formally deciding to go ahead with project
- starting the project communication process.

Planning the project involves:

- working out a project plan
- identifying risks and potential legal issues
- identifying a communication process
- preparing to document the project.

Implementing the project involves:

- carrying out the work needed to complete the project
- monitoring activities and tasks
- informing stakeholders of the project's progress.

Closing the project involves:

- finishing off any loose ends
- identifying follow-up activities
- preparing a summary project report
- disseminating the project outcomes
- formally closing the project.

The following case studies illustrate a number of different approaches to managing relatively simple projects. The first demonstrates the application of a traditional approach which was used in the introduction of family history workshops in a public library and this is followed by an adapted traditional approach as illustrated by the case studies on managing the content of a VLE, organising a conference, and a general approach to managing project.

Case study 2.1   Family history workshops

A public library in a small market town decided to introduce family history workshops. The professional librarian, Bushra, was asked to lead the project and deliver the workshops as she was experienced in family history. Table 2.1 on the next page illustrates how the actions Bushra took matched the stages of the project cycle.

Table 2.1 *Introduction of family history workshops*

Project cycle	Actions
Starting the project	
Produce project brief and justification	Bushra produced a one page summary of the proposed activity with justification (resources already available, there was an identified need for the service, it would increase library usage)
Make a formal decision to go ahead with the project	Customer services director decided to go ahead
Start the project communication process	Bushra informed all library staff about the project through team meetings; she decided that it was too early in the process to inform potential participants
Planning the project	
Work out a project plan with risk analysis and consideration for any legal issues	Bushra identified a suitable time slot (Thursday 10–12 a.m.) for the workshops; resources were available online; she booked the computers for the workshop
Identify risks and any potential legal issues	No special risks or legal issues identified, though participants were informed of standard health and safety practices and copyright issues at the start of each session
Identify communication process	Bushra produced a press release for the local press and a leaflet to display in the library and local supermarkets
Prepare to document the project	All documents kept on shared drive
Project implementation	
Carry out the work needed to complete the project	Bushra prepared handouts and an evaluation form for first session; she produced an introductory guide to the key databases available for family historians; 6 people attended the first session
Monitor activities and tasks	Feedback obtained from participants
Keep stakeholders informed of project and its progress	Bushra advised colleagues of the session before it took place and also of the feedback from the first session

Table 2.1 *Continued*

Closing the project	
Finish off any loose ends	None identified
Identify follow-up activities	Bushra identified sessions for the rest of the year and organised additional training for colleagues on using family history databases (so a larger team could deliver the sessions)
Prepare a summary project report	She produced a one page report recommending future activities
Disseminate the project	Bushra produced a press release
Close the project	She formally completed the project and told everyone that it is now part of the standard working practices in the library

Case study 2.2   Project management and the CILIP virtual learning environment

This case study was provided by Juanita Foster-Jones, Development Officer, Virtual Learning Environment (VLE) at CILIP in the UK. It demonstrates a slightly different approach to project management. Juanita is responsible for managing the content on the VLE – commissioning and project managing the development of content. She writes:

This requires project management skills to ensure that workload is balanced and prioritised, and that quality content is delivered in the most efficient and timely manner. Projects on the CILIP VLE fall under two categories:

1   Contracted content: where a third party is commissioned to develop content for CILIP for a set fee
2   Donated content: content is provided either by a special interest group, CILIP member or external party free of charge.

The project management approach for each category is slightly different, although there are some commonalities. We do not formally use PRINCE2® methodology in either case. Whilst this has value for large, formal projects where a clear audit trail and documentation is required, for small level projects with limited resources a much more flexible and reactive approach is required.

Contracted content

Project initiation: Projects are scoped via a project proposal which is judged by CILIP staff to see if it fits with the PKSB, is value for money, and will support member's professional development. Once agreed a contract is issued that defines what is being developed, the time scale for delivery and the fee to be paid. Dates are negotiated between the supplier and CILIP, to ensure that a suitable timescale is chosen. Suppliers are also briefed about VLE guidelines for developing content, and provided with support and guidance on learning design.

Managing project delivery: During the development of the content, the supplier works on the whole independently, with support and guidance provided as required via e-mail and phone. Once the content is delivered it is processed onto the VLE as soon as possible. For this there is no definite timeframe, as it is dependent on workload commitments. It is given priority where possible, and most importantly the supplier is kept informed of progress e.g. expected completion date, any hold-ups in the process. During the migration to the VLE there is an 'editing period' whereby the supplier provides commentary and approval of the content. The project management skills are in negotiating the timeframe with the supplier, managing workload, and liaising with other CILIP staff as required to develop the content.

Project closure: The project is finished once the course is complete on the VLE and the supplier has approved the final product. Promotion is the final stage once the course goes live, and articles, news features and postings on social media occur.

Donated content

Project initiation: This is more informal for donated content. Content is usually offered by the group/member and a discussion follows identifying whether it is suitable for the CILIP VLE and how it could be developed. If possible a timescale is identified, but where content is being developed on a voluntary basis this is not enforced.

Managing project delivery: This can be a complex process for donated content. Given that the supplier is doing this on a voluntary basis it is not possible to chase missed deadlines. Content can be agreed on, but then take over a year to be developed and delivered. This makes it difficult to manage as a project. Instead periodic e-mails are exchanged to ask for updates and expected time and offer support. When the content comes in it is developed as much as possible within existing workloads. As with contracted content, the supplier is kept informed of progress, and involved for editing and approval. In terms of project management skills there is much more emphasis on maintaining the relationship, and trying to provide an impetus so that progress occurs.

Project closure: This replicates the process for the contracted content.

Conclusion

Project management for the VLE is a more relaxed and reactive process than more formal methods of project management. There is no large team or budget, just the Development Officer, the supplier and possibly other CILIP staff who are brought in as required. As such the management is more to do with managing workload, the relationship, and providing a vision and guidance as to what is required of the CILIP VLE. It can be frustrating when you are waiting for donated content, but one has to remember that your project is just an extra in someone else's busy workload. But when the course is released to members it is all worthwhile.

Case study 2.3   Organising your first conference

A good example of a relatively simple project is organising a conference. There are many articles on organising a conference, and a particularly useful one is provided by Brewerton (2016) who writes from experience and has written the 'Meeting the reading list challenge' series. He organises his guide under the following headings:

- developing the draft programme
- finding a venue
- registration (with the example of using the online system Eventbrite)
- a month to go
- a few days before
- hosting the conference
- all over (until next time).

This is an extremely useful and readable guide.

Lisa Jeskins (see www.lisajeskinstraining.com) kindly provided me with this case study about her experiences of managing projects.

Case study 2.4   Project management: a view from a trainer and consultant

As a freelance trainer and consultant, a lot of what I do is managing projects. I've read quite a lot around the subject of project management and there are lots of models out there. It's a question of scale. If I was doing a large project working with a team, where I needed roles and responsibilities defined, then I might use PRINCE2®. If I was involved in developing something where we needed to be efficient but really responsive to changes, I might think about using Agile methodologies. For my own smaller projects where I'm managing lots of different tasks and different types of work for just me to do, practically I need a simpler tool.

In my mind project management is a cross between organisational skills and time management. Before you start work, you need to make sure you know what you are doing, how you are going to do it, how you will know when you've done it and how you are going to keep to your deadline. Project definition and preparation are the basis of good project management.

Do you understand properly what is required, what is the importance of it and what quality it needs to be? Taking the time to thoroughly understand what a project is meant to deliver is always time well spent. Actually doing the work can take less time if you have done your preparation properly and have developed a robust plan. Otherwise you can end up struggling to get started because your brief is too vague.

The first thing I do is work out what the aims and objectives are. This might mean talking to stakeholders and having conversations about what the project requirements are. Whilst you're talking about requirements and clarifying your understanding, you can iron out what the roles and responsibilities are too. Who do you go to, to ask questions? Who can help? Who understands the project and is invested in it? How and why are they invested in it? Sorting this out at the beginning can prevent misunderstanding later on.

Once you have your objectives you can divide these up into your tasks. Think about building a house. Your aim is the foundation, your objectives are the structural supports and then your tasks are the building blocks. Dividing a project up into individual jobs and tasks means that it feels achievable and you can divvy up the work between the project team and work out how long you need to do each job.

You also need to work out how perfect work needs to be as this can really add time to a project. Is perfection required or will good enough do? This will often depend on whether the project is public facing, who the stakeholders are? (Is it the big big boss?) Or if the project involves some sort of risk to the organisation or someone's health. You need to think about what needs to be included and what doesn't? How far are you going to go? You need to think about what might go wrong and how you can mitigate risk? Planning for possible issues is vital. Brainstorm worst case scenarios and what you would do. Staff sickness? Sudden budget reduction? Technology failure? Try and think of all possibilities. So if the zombie apocalypse does hit, you've got it covered.

The other key project management tip I've learned? Tasks almost always take longer than you've anticipated. Remember that this is the golden rule of any project and if possible see if you can add extra time to the timescales. Once you've done that, if you can, build in a deadline of your own, at least a week before the actual deadline. This is a luxury that you might not have but if you are in any way responsible for estimating timescales, I would build extra time into the project plan.

A colleague and I are working on a project at the moment. We have our deadline and the real deadline. We're both self-employed and this extra week allows for contingencies like sickness or other emergencies where we are unable to work and it allows us to check quality. This project is important and its success will be linked with our reputation and credibility. This means it's got to be great. An extra week will allow us to tweak, polish and perfect.

Depending on the scope and size of a project I might create a lot of documentation in order to prepare my aims, objectives and task lists. I might use Gantt charts to prepare my timelines and milestones. For the less formal and smaller projects, I have my trusty pukka pad full of all of my preparation and research and I create session outline documents.

Designing a bespoke training course for an organisation is an example of one of my smaller and more informal projects. In this instance I always create a session outline, which includes the aim and objectives for the session, details of what content will be imparted and what activities the delegates will complete. There will be a list of what flipcharts need to be prepared, what handouts need to be created and printed out and what resources are needed for the exercises, e.g. post-it notes, coloured pens, activity sheets etc. It also tells me how long I should take to discuss it or give people to do an exercise. I try and add an extra exercise in too, should my timings go awry. Prior to starting to design, I'll have had conversations with the person commissioning the training to find out if there are any problems that they think the training will solve and what they want people to know, feel and do afterwards. I use the answers to these questions as ways to prepare content and exercises but also to evaluate the training I create. What will success look like, e.g. staff who feel more confident dealing with difficult conversations?

It's a good idea to build in learning and reflection into your project plan so it isn't forgotten and to make sure you can improve how you work in future. The last part of your plan should include how you are going to evaluate the project and thinking around what success is, in terms of this project. How are you going to disseminate the results and what are your recommendations and suggestions for ongoing action and future work. I always explicitly state that I will list lessons learned to inform future projects. If you will, my last lesson learnt is to always include lessons learned.

Chapter 7 provides guidance on software that project managers who take a traditional approach to their project can use.

PRINCE2®

PRINCE2® (PRojects IN Controlled Environments) is a process-based methodology, which is widely used by the UK government and public sector, and the private sector. As with other approaches to project management, PRINCE2® identifies a series of stages or steps that are required to complete the project:

- starting up a project
- initiating a project
- directing a project
- controlling a stage
- managing product delivery
- managing a stage boundary
- closing a project.

PRINCE2® is commonly used in large and/or complex projects, and there are a number of key differences to the traditional approach. See Table 2.2 opposite, which outlines each of its stages.

Table 2.2 indicates some of the key features of the PRINCE2® methodology. First there is a formal management structure for the project. Figure 2.3 on page 34 presents a complex project (sometimes called a programme) in which the board (led by the project sponsor or executive) directs the work of three sub-projects, each led by a project manager who works with a team dedicated to that particular aspect of the programme. The board's membership is likely to include appropriate senior staff, e.g. directors of service, as well as the project manager(s). Their role is to lead and steer the project, and to approve key decisions throughout the project process.

Table 2.2 *Typical activities commonly undertaken during the different stages of a PRINCE2® project*

Stage	Typical activities
Starting up a project	Establish project board Appoint project sponsor or executive Appoint project management team Prepare project brief Identify project approach Prepare business case Review lesson logs from previous projects Plan the next stage
Initiating a project	Produce project plan Develop a more detailed business case including risks and potential legal issues Plan quality Set up project controls Set up project documentation process
Directing a project	The project board is responsible for approving the project and its initiation, authorising any exceptions, monitoring the budget, giving feedback and advice to project management team, formally closing project
Controlling a stage	Includes all activities or work packages that take place within a particular stage of the project; the project management team is responsible for approving work packages, assessing progress, identifying issues, monitoring and controlling risks, reviewing stage status, taking corrective action, escalating issues e.g. to the board, reporting highlights to the programme board and other stakeholders, receiving completed work packages
Managing product delivery	The project manager works with the project workers or team, who accept a work package, complete the work, and deliver the work package to the manager
Managing a stage boundary	Towards the end of a stage: plan the next stage, update the project plan, update the business case and risk register, report stage end, and if necessary produce an exceptions plan
Closing a project	Formally end the project, identify follow-up actions, produce a benefits review plan and a project evaluation review

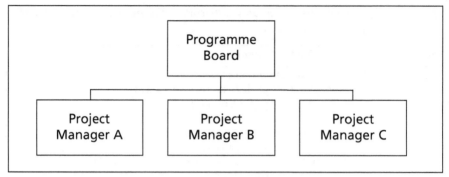

Figure 2.3 *Diagram showing the project leadership and management structure*

Second, PRINCE2® requires that everything is carefully documented at every stage of the project so every decision and details of all project activities are carefully documented and reported, as appropriate to the project manager and/or project board. This makes it very easy to track the project and its development, and ensures that if there is a change in project staff the new arrival will be able to identify the current status of the project quickly.

The third key feature of PRINCE2® is that the project is divided into specific stages, each of which involves a number of work packages (which may be divided into a number of tasks) with identifiable outputs (Figures 2.4 and 2.5).

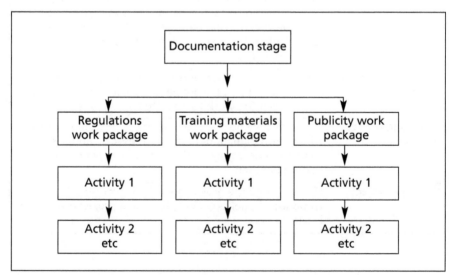

Figure 2.4 *Example project stage made up of three work packages*

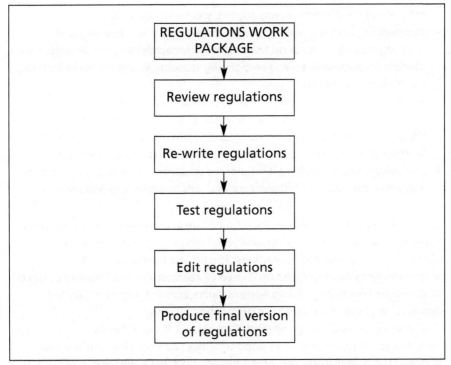

Figure 2.5 *Example project work package made up of five distinct activities*

Case study 2.5   Learning Futures

In my role of pro-vice-chancellor and dean, I was involved in a major change programme, Learning Futures, at the University of Westminster in London. This was a strategic, large-scale (university-wide), complex project with a budget of more than £2.4 million. The three-year programme aimed to transform the undergraduate experience and was managed using PRINCE2® methodology. A programme board chaired by a member of the university's executive team directed Learning Futures. The programme was made up of four projects, each of which was led by a senior academic who chaired the project boards. Membership of the project boards reflected the university community, and included students, professional services staff and academics. The four projects were:

- *curriculum and assessment* – changing the academic framework and assessment regulations; the university had another major project working alongside the Learning Futures programme aimed at developing the academic information system so the changes, e.g. to the structure of degree

programmes and academic regulations, were embedded in it
- *transforming learning and teaching* – developing a new learning and teaching strategy, a focus on teaching skills for academics, the development of learning communities, and recognising students as co-creators in learning, teaching and research
- *Westminster distinctiveness* – defining graduate attributes that were then embedded in the redesigned undergraduate curriculum, developing Westminster electives to enhance cross-disciplinary learning, and setting up Westminster Distinctiveness Awards for extra-curriculum achievements
- *academic support* – making it simpler for students to find and access support, and enhancing skills and support for students to become lifelong learners.

The project as a whole was managed by a professional project leader who line managed the individual project managers. Each project manager had the support of one or two project workers. The project team included a communications manager who facilitated all communications about the project to the wider community and an administrative assistant. Figure 2.6 on the opposite page shows the structure of Learning Futures.

The advantages of using the PRINCE2® approach were that there was a very clear project structure, roles and responsibilities were clearly identified and documented, and the progress of the project (and any issues) was well documented and very easy to track. Members of the professional project team working on the project were well qualified in project management tools and techniques, which was their sole responsibility. Therefore they helped to keep the momentum of the project going even at busy times, e.g. enrolment and induction. The project team members were all employed on short-term contracts as the life of the whole programme was three years; there were some changes in personnel as they chose to move to other projects. However, the quality of the documentation enabled new recruits to get to grips with their new role quickly. Another advantage of working with a team of professional project managers was that knowledge and skills of project management were disseminated across the students, professional support staff and academics who were directly working on the project, e.g. as board members.

My perception of the disadvantages of using the PRINCE2® approach was that sometimes the programme and individual projects appeared to be over-documented, and that at some meetings time was spent going through material on activities that had been completed. There appeared to be repetition, e.g. between individual project board meetings and the programme board meetings. At one stage, I found a project worker attempting to document an informal meeting which had taken place and had resulted in the

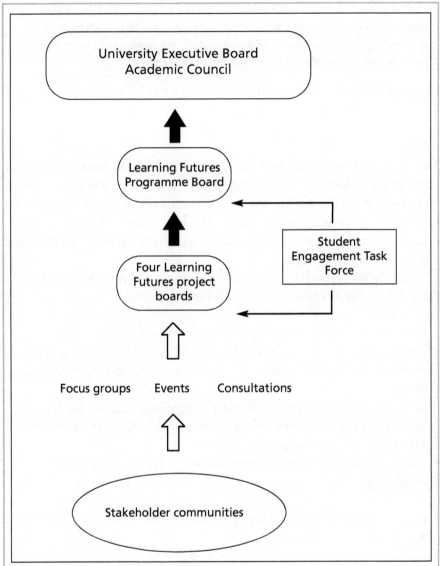

Figure 2.6 *The structure of Learning Futures*

desired outcome. She found it frustrating to be asked not to spend time on this activity and I found it frustrating that she wanted to spend time retrospectively documenting an informal meeting, which resulted in a task being completed to everyone's satisfaction.

Overall, the use of PRINCE2® enabled a very large-scale and complex project to be professionally managed so that it achieved its outcomes. The project methodology and its approach to documentation ensured that changes in personnel – students, professional support staff, academics and the project team – did not adversely affect the success of the project.

Lawton (2015) provides a simple introduction to PRINCE2® and Chapter 7 provides guidance on relevant software.

Agile

The Agile approach to project management, which is commonly used in software and information technology (IT) projects, developed in the 1970s as a reaction to the traditional top-down (sometimes called waterfall) approaches to project management. The key feature of Agile is that it enables teams to respond to changing requirements through incremental and iterative project work.

A common approach to Agile involves sprints and scrums, described in Table 2.3 on the next page, with the following teams:

- *development team* – the group of people working on the product
- *product owner* – the person responsible for ensuring that the product meets the customer's needs, who works with the development team daily
- *scrum master* (or project facilitator) – the person responsible for supporting the development team, resolving blocks and ensuring that the Agile process is followed
- *stakeholders* – the people with an interest in the project and its product(s).

Projects managed using an Agile approach are well documented and the following are commonly used:

- *a product vision statement* – a summary used to communicate the product and its value to the organisation
- *a product backlog* – the list of what is in the scope of the project in priority order
- *a product roadmap* – a high-level view of the product with an associated loose time frame for its development
- *a release plan* – a high-level timetable for the release of working aspects of the product

- *sprint backlog* – a sprint is a particular cycle of work and the sprint backlog is the goal and tasks associated with the current sprint
- *increment* – the working product functionality at the end of each sprint.

Table 2.3 *The Agile process*

Stages	Activities
Vision	The product owner identifies the vision for the new or revised product, defining the product, its relationship with the organisation's strategy, and who will use it.
Product roadmap	A high-level view of the product requirements and a loose time frame for its development
Release plan	The high-level timetable for releasing the working software; it may be in stages
Sprint planning	A short cycle of development lasting from 1 day to 4 weeks that results in a specific product; the product owner, master and development team plan 'sprints', which are also called iterations; they start creating the product within these sprints, each of which starts with a planning session where the development team identify the requirements for that stage of the product
Daily scrum	During each sprint, the development team meets daily; these may be short meetings, sometimes called scrums, focusing on what team members did yesterday, what they will do today, any issues
Sprint review	Held at the end of every sprint, with a demonstration of the product developed during that sprint to stakeholders
Sprint retrospective	A meeting held at the end of every sprint where team members discuss the success of the sprint and plans for improvements in the next sprint

Case study 2.6   Mobile website

Critchlow, Friedman and Suchy (2011) describe how the University of California San Diego Libraries developed and implemented a mobile website using an Agile approach to the project. A team, the Mobile Advisory Group, consisted of four representatives from User Services groups, a facilitator and the web technical manager; they worked within a two month timeframe. These were the key features of the project:

- a short, well-structured timeline in three two-week cycles
- extensive communications face to face and via chat and social media

- an awareness that a traditional project management top-down approach with multiple committee meetings was not appropriate when dealing with a rapidly changing area
- a small team given authority to decide and design on behalf of the entire organisation
- an understanding that sometimes fast and 'good enough' is better than slow and perfect.

In their conclusion, Critchlow, Friedman and Suchy (2011) state:

Overall, this project and process have garnered positive feedback from users and library administration, and we envision employing a similar approach to development projects in the future. However, it is important to note that this is obviously not a panacea for project management in general, as certain characteristics limit what can be accomplished. This model is most appropriate for projects with:

- Small to medium scope
- Key staff available for a short duration of significant workload
- Support of library administration in allowing the representatives to make decisions on behalf of all the stakeholders
- Timeliness and rapid development as a crucial factor for success

Conversely, it might not be a good model for projects with:

- Enterprise level scope
- Dependencies on campus or consortia-wide involvement
- The need to include and consider feedback from every stakeholder
- A lack of firm administrative support.

Case study 2.7   Development of a virtual research environment

Enright and Summers (2014) describe the use of an Agile approach at the University of Westminster, in developing a virtual research environment (VRE) to support PhD candidates throughout their research, manage and document the research ethics approval process for students and staff, and streamline the outputs from research projects. They write:

The VRE provides us with a very flexible platform upon which we can quickly develop new functionality to help our researchers as new requirements emerge. By working collaboratively with users, we increased the chance of creating the right solution, and our users developed an early sense of ownership and engagement with the project which helped ensure a successful deployment.

Traditionally, many Library and Information Services may have deployed new services in one big bang, delaying until all the elements of the new service were ready. A more agile, flexible, and responsive approach is particularly useful for services in new areas where requirements are emerging and evolving. It may at first seem more risky, but it enables you to test and tweak your approach as you go along. Ultimately, this gives you a much better chance of delivering a service that really meets the needs of your users.

Finally, Chapter 7 provides guidance on software which may be used by project managers who take an Agile approach to their project. A useful guide to Agile has been written by Cole and Scotcher (2015).

Selecting an approach to project management

At the start of a project it is important to select the best approach to project management for your project. Table 2.4 on the following page, lists various criteria to consider when choosing, showing which of the three approaches (traditional, PRINCE2® or Agile) is most suitable for different sorts of project. Use this table to help you decide which approach is most suitable for your project.

The next step is to explore the approaches in more detail and discuss them with colleagues, including those with project management experience. You will then need to make a final decision about your project approach or methodology.

The people side of projects

All projects, whether small or large, have an impact on a wide range of people, including library and information workers, senior managers, the professional project management team, colleagues from other disciplines e.g. IT specialists, stakeholders, project partners, project funders, allies and champions – and the library and information community. An essential aspect of project management is to establish and maintain effective two-way communications processes to ensure that there is support for the project and its outcomes. The different groups of people involved are considered below.

Table 2.4 *Criteria for choosing an approach to project management*

	Traditional approach	PRINCE2® (or similar methodology)	Agile (or similar approach)	Your project
Project involves strategic change	X	X		
Project involves operational change	X	X	X	
Project involves many stakeholders who need to be considered at every stage		X		
Project is complex	X	X		
Project is relatively simple	X		X	
Project involves several partner organisations		X		
Project involves rapid technological change			X	

Library and information workers

Small or simple projects may be carried out by an individual or small team who are deeply committed to its success. In contrast, large and complex projects may require a wide range of staff with varying degrees of commitment to the project. Project managers may have no choice over the selection of team or committee members, so they often have to work with colleagues who range from people with appropriate knowledge, skills, interest and enthusiasm for the project to others who are de-motivated and unenthusiastic. The project manager is responsible for getting this potentially wide range of colleagues to work together as a team and deliver the required project outcomes.

The project manager and team need to consider how to engage with all library and information workers, whether or not they are directly working on the project, and be kept informed and consulted as the project develops. Those staff who are not directly involved in the project may have taken on additional work while it is in progress, e.g. cover for some of the project team members, so their work should be acknowledged and validated. This is particularly true in high-profile projects where 'fame and fortune' may be linked to the project manager and team workers while the staff who maintain the library service are not acknowledged for their contributions. If this type of division arises it can lead to resentment and bad feeling between different groups of staff.

Senior managers

Support from senior managers who may be library and information professionals or from different professions is vital to the success of the project. In large and complex projects, senior managers are likely to be members of the project board. In small or simple projects, it is likely that they are the people who will approve the project and its budget. It is important to ensure that you have their support and that you keep them informed of the project progress and outcomes.

Professional project management team

Many organisations now employ professional project managers and team workers either permanently or on short-term contracts. Permanent staff are an intrinsic part of your organisation but if your project employs contract staff then work with your human resources department to ensure that the recruitment and selection process runs smoothly. There should be an induction process for contract staff (as with any new recruit) and they require access to the same performance management and staff development processes as do staff on permanent contracts. This issue is considered in more detail in Chapter 9.

Colleagues from other disciplines

It is very rare for library and information service projects not to involve working with colleagues from other disciplines, e.g. IT specialists, web team members, educational development staff, and buildings and estates staff. Working in multi-professional teams is interesting as sometimes our basic assumptions and approaches to a problem may be challenged, and it provides access to a wide range of ideas and perspectives. However, more time needs to be spent on building the team and developing a shared understanding of the project, its aim and outcomes, and working practices than when working on a project with a single profession team.

Project partners

Collaborative projects involve working with partner institutions, which may be located in different countries. The funding for collaborative partnerships often includes a budget for face-to-face meetings, which may take place at the beginning of the project and then as it reaches each of its milestones. In between, project managers and team members communicate via e-mail, tools such as Skype or FaceTime, and social media. Again, it is well worth spending time getting to know partners and to use face-to-face or telephone communication if problems arise. The theme of working in diverse teams and in partnership is considered in chapters 9 and 10.

Project funders

If a project is externally funded it is important to get to know the funders and their requirements. Take any opportunities possible to meet them. A key aspect of working with funding organisations is to follow their reporting and communications procedures. If you wish to change any aspect of the project, gain written permission for any changes. Maintain positive communications with the funding organisation and the people funding your project. This will help your project achieve its outcomes and may also help you to be successful in future funding bids.

Stakeholders

The project stakeholders are all the people who have a specific interest and investment in the library and information service, the project and its outcomes. They may be located within or outside your organisation, for example customers, suppliers, sponsors and colleagues within and outside the library service who are not working on the projects. At a very early stage in the project it is worth spending time identifying your stakeholders and considering their potential level of involvement, so you can decide to what extent to keep them informed: through consultation or direct inclusion in the project work. It is well worth investing time in building up these relationships and creating effective communication channels with stakeholders. These people are likely to be important allies and can cause major problems if they are ignored or treated thoughtlessly.

Allies and champions

Allies and champions are the people who will support and champion your project so identify and get to know them. Formal project management methodologies, such as PRINCE2®, involve a formal project sponsor who chairs the project board and is likely to be a member of the senior management team. Whatever approach to project management you use, find a champion at a senior level, as this person is likely to help you resolve problems or other issues that arise during the life of the project. Spending some time identifying and building up your relationship with your allies and champions and enhancing their knowledge of the project is likely to be time well spent.

The wider library and information profession
Whatever the size of your project, it is likely to be of interest to other library and information workers who are working on or likely to be implementing similar projects across the world, and members of the library and information community are often very willing to share their experiences and expertise. If you are actively involved in the library networks relevant to your work you will find that they provide many opportunities for exchanging ideas. In contrast, at the end of your project you may find it helpful to disseminate your findings and experiences through the professional literature, meetings or conferences

Chapters 3 to 6 consider the different stages of a project and the importance of working with and managing the different groups of people outlined above and communicating throughout the project process. Chapter 9 considers the people side of projects in more detail and covers topics such as: fundamental requirements for project workers, developing working practices, working in diverse and virtual teams, working with volunteers, crowdsourcing and change management.

The management of change is an important consideration for anyone involved in strategic projects. Large and complex projects result in major changes occurring during the life of the project or as a result of its outcomes. Changes that take place may include:

- change in work location
- change in role and job description
- change in working practices
- change in line management
- change in team membership and working practices
- new contracts of employment.

The project manager might consider using change management tools and techniques, as individuals respond to change and uncertainty in many different ways. Some embrace change and see it as an opportunity for development or advancement; others want to stay with the previous approaches to work. As a project leader or manager be aware of individuals' and teams' responses to change and be prepared to manage any ensuring impacts. In some organisations, the human resources department contains a specialist team responsible for managing change and working with teams as strategic changes are introduced across the institution. Increasingly, many projects involve working in partnership, e.g. with libraries in the same or different sector, and with public or sector organisations such as businesses, voluntary organisations or funding bodies. It is helpful to develop robust relationships with these partners. This topic is considered in Chapter 10.

Summary

This chapter gave an overview of project management by considering the project approach or methodology, the people side of projects, and the management of change. The three approaches to project management considered are a traditional approach, PRINCE2® and Agile. Each approach has its own merits and is relevant to different types of projects. The people side of projects should be taken into consideration if the project is to be successful. This is considered in more detail in Chapters 9 and 10.

This chapter described the many different groups of people who need to be considered by the project manager and team: library and information workers, the professional project management team, colleagues from other disciplines e.g. IT specialists, stakeholders, project partners, project funders, allies and champions, and the wider library and information community. Finally, the importance of change management was outlined in the context of strategic or major projects.

References

APM (2016) *Don't Get Left Behind*, apm.org.uk.

Brewerton, G. (2016) Organising Your First Conference, *Ariadne*, **76**, www.ariadne.ac.uk/issue/76/brewerton/.

Cole, R. and Scotcher, E. (2015) *Brilliant Agile Project Management: a practical guide to using Agile, Scrum and Kanban*, Pearson Education.

Critchlow, M., Friedman, L. G. and Suchy, D. (2011) *Using an Agile-based Approach to Develop a Library Mobile Website: the university libraries,* https://escholarship.org/uc/item/38d937jr/.

Enright, S. and Summers, J. (2014) *The Agile Library: developing services for researchers,* www.infotoday.eu/Authors/Suzanne-Enright-and-Jennifer-Summers-6705.aspx/.

Lawton, I. (2015) *PRINCE2® Made Simple,* P2MS Press.

CHAPTER 3

Getting started

Introduction

This chapter outlines all the activities that need to take place before the project gains approval and can go ahead. Working through them when you are at the start of a potential project can help ensure that you get off to a good start.

At this early stage in the project process, think about defining the proposed project, the project leadership and management structures, and the people side of projects including team work and communications. Then think about technical aspects such as risk analysis, legal issues, finance, and project documentation. The result of this work is a project brief, a short written summary of the proposed project, which is then used to gain formal approval for the project.

Project initiation

Projects are initiated in many different ways: when developing a new strategy for the library service or introducing new technologies; following changes in the environment or funding; a crisis; or through personal interest. For example, a number of new library buildings have been developed in universities in response to changing demands and expectations of their student population. Many libraries have developed services that are accessible using new mobile technologies. Many public libraries have developed and implemented shared services as a result of financial pressures. In contrast, sometimes a library or information worker has a good idea during the course of their everyday work, in discussions with colleagues or as a result of attending a conference, and this then forms the basis of a project.

Coffin and Morrill (2015) discuss a model to promote innovation in Wisconsin Library Services (WiLS), a membership organisation involving over 600 libraries in Wisconsin USA, and their model helps to transform creative ideas into sound projects. They suggest that innovative projects have the following characteristics:

- are based on need and its potential impact
- have clear measures of success
- take into account conventions and norms
- are iterative
- provide a basis for organisational growth and learning.

They conclude:

> Innovation is rarely fully borne in a lightbulb moment. Innovative services require time and effort and thought to plan, launch, and refine until they become truly responsive and effective. And even once a project has reached that point, it still needs ongoing adjustment to respond to shifts in needs and means. That is, innovative ideas require at least a little trial and error. Error is scary to publicly-supported institutions like libraries because it suggests the possibility of wasted resources. We believe this model helps reduce that risk, fosters experimentation in library endeavours, and encourages those experiments to grow into useful and effective services with meaningful and lasting effects on the community.
>
> (Coffin and Morrill, 2015, 28)

Sometimes the idea for a project comes from outside the library and information service, for example as part of a strategic change in the parent organisation or as a response to a changing external environment. For instance, in response to financial pressures the local authority in the rural East Riding of Yorkshire refurbished a number of libraries located in small towns or large villages and moved their customer services staff into these libraries so they were able to offer a wide range of services. This change helped to ensure that public libraries remained open and accessible in a large rural county.

Frequently, the initial idea for a project is followed up through research, e.g. into the user group, who may benefit from the project. This is illustrated in the following study by Caperon (2015) which is followed by two sets of resources which focus on building a new library and moving a library.

Case study 3.1   Developing adaptable, efficient mobile library services: librarians as enablers

Caperon (2015) uses a grounded theory approach to research users' need for mobile library services at the University of Leeds. Grounded theory involves working from the concepts and ideas of the participants rather than those of the researchers. Caperon used a combination of qualitative and quantitative methods – focus groups and online questionnaires – to explore users' needs. Her approach to analysing the data included the use of axial coding (common in grounded theory research) to identify core themes from the qualitative data. The results from the online questionnaires showed that users would be most likely to use their mobile devices for the following activities (in order of preference):

- renew books
- check a library account
- find library open hours, locations or phone numbers
- search for books in the catalogue
- reserve books
- search for articles in a library database
- search for e-books in the catalogue
- read or view online articles or books
- use library research guides and tutorials.

The focus groups evaluated the university's institutional app and identified potential improvements to it. They considered other services such as text messaging and the value of QR (Quick Response) codes, which are two-dimensional barcodes that can be read using smartphones and typically store URLs or other information, e.g. guidance to students on a range of resources, then as a result of this research created a mobile services toolkit in the library. Finally, Caperon recognises that this is a rapidly developing field so the results will become out of date quickly.

This study demonstrates how important it is to research users' needs thoroughly to inform the development of a project at an early stage.

Resources on building a new library

New library builds are a good example of large-scale and complex projects. Some library and information service directors and managers are in the fortunate position of building a new library, normally a once in a lifetime opportunity. Fortunately, there is an incredible range of resources available to help them lead and project manage the new build. Although these resources tend not to include the detailed project management tools and techniques covered in this book, they give valuable insights into the particular challenges and issues of building a new library.

One particularly useful free resource is the website Designing Libraries (http://designinglibraries.org.uk). It provides a vast range of resources, including guides on topics such as:

- managing a successful library design and furnishing project
- planning a successful library or archive move
- designing libraries and learning centres for good acoustics
- how to photograph your library.

These are some useful resources:

- Design Council (2008) *Inclusion by Design: equality, diversity and the built environment*, www.designcouncil.org.uk/resources/guide/inclusion-design-equality-diversity-and-built-environment.
- Harrison, A. and Hutton, L. (2013) *Landscape: space, place and the future of learning*, Routledge.
- Khan, A. (2008) *Better by Design: an introduction to planning and designing a new library building*, Facet Publishing.
- Miller, R. T. and Genco, B. A. (2015) *Better Library Design: ideas from library journal*, Rowman and Littlefield.
- University of Cambridge (2015) *Inclusive Design Tool Kit*, www.inclusivedesigntoolkit.com.

Resources on moving a library
There are many helpful resources available for those starting a library move project. Although they tend not to include the project management tools and techniques covered in this book, they provide detailed guidance and examples of good practices and the challenges of moving a library:

- Bendix, C. (2013) *Moving Collections*, British Library, www.bl.uk.
- Benitez-Eves, T. (2013) Making the Right Move, *Library Journal*, http:lj.libraryjournal.com.
- Cash, D. (2012) Moving a Library Collection, *Public Library Quarterly*, **20** (4), 17–28.
- Fortriede, S. C. (2010) *Moving your Library: getting the collection from here to there*, American Library Association.
- Hitchcock, M., Sager, R. and Schneider, J. (2005) And Then There Was One:

moving and merging three health science library collections, *Science and Technology Librarianship*, www.istl.org.

Articles and reports of this kind often give detailed guidance on planning a move and useful tips on the reality of such a project.

Defining the project

Defining the project involves identifying the overall aim of the project and what must be achieved – the project outcomes. The aim is something that people will work towards and be motivated by. It should be aligned with the vision, mission and strategic plan of the library and information service. To turn the aim into a reality it is necessary to identify the project's intended outcomes. It is very important that the project's aim and intended outcomes are aligned with those of the library and information service otherwise the proposed project will result in a diversion of staff time and resources from the main work of the service and its parent organisation.

Identify the scope of the project. Many projects start off with a narrowly defined scope and in a small pilot or research phase, which – depending on its success – later expands. For example, the initial scope of a project on the design and development of learning materials was limited to developing three basic resources. Once these had been produced and the project evaluated the scope was broadened to include another subject area. Identifying what is outside the scope of the project helps to develop a tight project boundary, which helps prevent unplanned project expansion – the growth of the project leading to a pressure on resources and missed deadlines.

The timescale of the project needs to be considered too. What are the proposed start and end dates? How do these fit in with the library service requirements? What might be the impact of seasonal variations in the workload of the library staff? It is worth identifying some project 'milestones': key landmarks in the project process. Two obvious milestones are the project start and end dates. In a project involving moving a library, milestones could include end of weeding of stock, end of updating catalogue records, all periodicals moved to new location, or all books moved to new location.

Milestones are important as they can be motivators to staff, who can see how progress is made as they are passed. They provide useful measures for evaluating and celebrating the success of a project throughout the project process.

At the project planning stage resourcing requirements of the project should be considered. There is no need to carry out a detailed staffing or budget analysis at this stage, but some general indication of the costs and where staff resources and budget will come from is necessary. It is also worth thinking about whether or not you will require additional ICT resources.

Once you have begun to define the project it is helpful to research and identify library and information services that have carried out similar work so you can learn from their experiences. Useful sources of information include professional networks, conferences, discussion lists and colleagues.

At this stage it is worth producing a brief summary of your work. Table 3.1 shows a typical format for this initial project definition to use as a starting point for further discussions with colleagues.

Project stakeholders

Chapter 2 introduced the wide range of stakeholders who may be involved

Table 3.1 *A brief project summary*

Topic	Summary notes
Working project title	
Project aim	
Project outcomes	
Scope	
Timescale	
Milestones	
Resource requirements – people	
Resource requirements – ICT	
Resource requirements – other	
Brief summary of research on contemporary similar projects	
Other notes	

in library and information service projects, for example library and information workers, senior managers, professional project management team, colleagues from other disciplines e.g. IT specialists, stakeholders, project partners, project funders, allies and champions, and the library and information community. At this early stage in the life of the project, it is worth identifying the people who are likely to work on it, e.g. as a result of working in the library or as a customer.

King (2013) carried out a stakeholder analysis for a project that assessed research services at the University of North Carolina Libraries, distinguishing individuals and groups who would be responsible and accountable for the project, and consulted and informed about it:

- *responsible* – those responsible for completing particular tasks, e.g. members of the project team
- *accountable* – those responsible if the task is not completed, and the project manager responsible for monitoring the project schedule
- *consulted* – those not responsible or accountable for completing tasks or the project as a whole, but who have a stake in the operation of the reference services, e.g. co-workers and student workers; consulted when necessary in one-to-one meetings
- *informed* – those not responsible or accountable for the completion of tasks or the project as a whole, but need to be kept informed; kept up to date with project developments. Those in the consulted category may also be in the informed category.

Table 3.2 on the next page lists different project stakeholders and their types of interaction with a project.

Case study 3.2   Building a new library

Demco Interiors for Designing Libraries (2012) provides a very useful planning guide that advises readers to consult widely throughout the planning and design process to ensure that the new library takes into account feedback from stakeholders rather than be based on assumptions of the project management team members. Librarians may carry out the consultations themselves or use the services of one of the suppliers. Demco Interiors for Designing Libraries (2012) describes the principles behind consultation as:

- Engaging stakeholders in the design process
- Listening to end users through creative workshops
- Working with library teams, partners and library users
- Fulfilling the consultation process to meet funding requirements
- Analysis and feedback for actionable conclusions
- Creating a relevant library interior, based on feedback.

Demco Interiors for Designing Libraries (2012) suggests that co-creation processes – working with stakeholders to create the library design – may involve developing 3D visualisations, sketch-ups and walk-throughs.

Table 3.2 *Project stakeholders and their types of interaction with a project*

Stakeholder	Type of interaction: responsible (R) accountable (A) consulted (C) informed (I)	Initial list of people needed to work on project
Senior leaders and managers		
Library service colleagues		
Professional project management team		
Colleagues from other disciplines		
Other stakeholders, e.g. customers		
Project partners		
Project funders		
Allies and champions		
Library and information community		

When introducing a technological change in a project it is necessary to decide how to structure that project: introduce the change to a pilot group first, or go for the 'big bang' approach and expect everyone to start using the new technology at the same time? Rogers (1983) provides a model for the spread of innovative ideas and technology, calculating the extent to which five groups start using a new idea or technology: innovators (2.5%), early adopters (13.5%), early majority (34%), late majority (34%) and laggards (16%). The next case study illustrates how early adopters can be recruited to pilot a project.

Case study 3.3   Introducing an online reading list system in an academic library

Ann Munn, Collections Management Team Leader at the University of Westminster, provided the following outline of the project to introduce an online reading list system in the library:

> The aims of the project were to procure and implement an online reading list and digitised content management system which would integrate with the University's library discovery software, VLE and the University's authentication systems. By following guidance from our IT project office, PRINCE2® methodology was used. MS Project was used but only in a simple way, as in producing a timeline for each of the work packages. Resource scheduling was not used because there were no dedicated resources. The pilot project ran from May 2014 to September 2015.
>
> The project approach was to deliver in two phases with an early adopter's phase going live in January 2015 and a second adopter's phase starting in May 2015 with a goal of 450 lists for semester one going live in September 2015.
>
> The University of Westminster's Services Evaluation Framework mandated an externally hosted service. Two companies fulfilled this requirement, PTFS Europe with Rebus: List and Talis with Talis Aspire and Talis Digitised Content. Both products were evaluated by product demonstrations and the response to a requirements specification. Talis was chosen.
>
> The project team consisted of members from all library teams, Academic Liaison Librarians, Collections Management team, Frontline team, as well as an Educational Technologist, the Systems Librarian and a member of the Communications team. The project team met monthly, risks and issues were recorded and assessed, as was progress against a work schedule. Work packages included integration with the VLE and the library's discovery software Library Search, workflow analysis, recruitment of early adopters, training and communications plan, gathering feedback from early adopters, second adopters phase and development of a support structure for business as usual. The Project Board consisted of a senior academic, the Associate Director of Library and Archive Services and the Head of Education Technology.

Negotiation of workflow changes was the main challenge. Who would do the inputting of reading lists? Librarians or academics? If librarians input lists then it was thought more likely that lists would be created. If academic staff input lists then ownership would be with them and it would be clear that ongoing maintenance and updating would be their responsibility. A mixture of approaches was tried at the different campuses. There was no agreement on what worked best, and approaches at each site remain different. A subsidiary aim of the project was to move ordering decisions related to reading lists away from the Academic Liaison Librarians to be driven by academic staff via the online system.

The online reading lists were made available via the VLE. The project achieved a change of workflow with most purchases of books being directly driven via the reading lists. Two hundred and sixty lists were available at the end of the project, falling short of the ambitious target of four hundred and fifty. Four months later the number of lists exceeded six hundred.

Some of the lessons learned:

- There was initial resistance to the implementation of online reading lists by some members of library staff. There should have been more emphasis on the benefits from the start of the project.
- The creation of an advocacy and training plan which was visible to all library staff and populated by the academic liaison librarians encouraged everyone by showing progress. By the end of the project there were 380 meetings and training events recorded. These could be group training or 1 to 1 sessions.

Project leadership and management structures

Project managers need to think about how they will manage a project and the systems and structures required to support them and the project. The case study above, 'Introducing an online reading list system in an academic library', illustrated a relatively simple structure involving a project board and project team. When starting a project think about the most appropriate structure for it, depending on the size and complexity of your project. On small and simple projects, the project may be led by a librarian as part of their normal workload. There is no need for a project management structure and the librarian reports project progress to her line manager and shares information about the project with co-workers.

When working on a large or complex project it is well worth involving at least three different groups of staff in the project process: a steering group, the management group and the project team. The project manager will be a member of all three groups and individual project team members, e.g. people with a particular expertise, may also be members of the management team. This is illustrated in Figure 3.1 below and Table 3.3 on the next page. If you are working on a project using a particular approach, e.g. PRINCE2® or Agile, these project methodologies use specified management structures, which are described in Chapter 2.

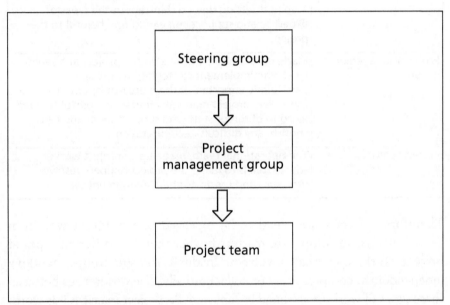

Figure 3.1 *The management structure of a project*

Project team work

At the start of a project it is essential to think about the type of team work required within a project as different types of project are best managed by organising and managing teams in different ways. Traditional library and information work often involves 'process' teams where people undertake routine and standardised activities or tasks. This is the most common form of work. It is repetitive, standardised, takes place over a predictable time period, and maintains the status quo. In contrast, project work is often less predictable, requires innovation, may be non-standardised, and results in change.

Table 3.3 *Typical characteristics of the project groups that manage large-scale or complex projects*

Project group	Characteristics
Steering group	Identifies the strategy for the project and ensures that it is aligned with that of the organisation and library; makes key decisions, e.g. formally approves the project and project budget; steers direction of project if there are major difficulties; group often involves a range of stakeholders who champion the project in various arenas; if setting one up think about the types of expertise and support you would find helpful to the project
Project management group	Made up of people involved in the project at a senior level who implement strategies; the group is particularly important if there are significant problems to resolve; project managers find it very useful to have a group of senior staff who support them and can confirm any difficult decisions taken
Project team	The operational team, made up of project workers, whose role is to make the project happen, resolve problems and report to the management team

Therefore project teams need to be managed in a different way from process teams. To complicate matters further there are different types of project work; they may involve individuals (or sub-groups) working independently, co-operatively or collaboratively. The differences between these types of work are outlined in Table 3.4. As project manager it is worth spending some time thinking about the best type of approach to project work for your team.

Table 3.4 *Different types of team work*

	Independent	Co-operative	Collaborative
Definition	Individuals work by themselves on their own tasks and have individual goals	Tasks are divided into parts and individuals are responsible for their own piece of work; they work together to ensure that the parts will work together; they have individual goals	The team works together on tasks; they share the tasks fluidly and work towards a shared goal

Table 3.4 *Continued*

	Independent	Co-operative	Collaborative
Types of tasks	Organising room bookings; acting as a contact person	Writing a project report; moving a library; developing a new ICT system	Producing a project plan; writing a project report; moving a library; developing a new ICT system
Effective project management patterns	Individuals are briefed and deadlines are agreed; individuals report to the project manager and/or team meetings; ICT is used to exchange information	The whole team is briefed and deadlines are agreed; division of work is agreed; boundaries between tasks are clarified; individuals agree how they will work together and deal with critical issues; ICT is used to support co-operative working	The whole team is briefed and deadlines are agreed; general division of work is agreed; individuals agree how they will work together; future meeting dates are set for collaborative work to take place; ICT is used to support collaborative working

Sometimes project managers assume that their project team will work either co-operatively or collaboratively when their specific project is best suited to people working independently. This is demonstrated in the next case study.

Case study 3.4   Identifying working practices in a cataloguing project

A number of years ago, I ran a workshop on team building at which one of the delegates outlined problems he was experiencing within his workplace library. He was leading a retrospective cataloguing project and found it difficult to get staff to attend and contribute to project meetings. He said, 'All they want to do is get on with the work and they hate coming to meetings.' After some discussion it became clear that the team members were all working extremely effectively on their allocated tasks and reported directly back to their project manager. There was no real need for them to meet each other and discuss their progress, although to some extent this happened informally over the photocopier. The project manager was attempting to lead team meetings when they were not really required. Once he had explored the different patterns of team working within a project he realised that it was probably more effective to manage the individuals working on the project rather than attempt to lead the project via team meetings.

Project communications

A common feature of successful projects is that the project communication process has been thought through and planned in some detail at the start of the project. It is worth thinking about who is going to be responsible for the project communication process and how it is going to be managed. Think in broad terms about the answers to the following questions:

- Who will be responsible for developing the project communications strategy?
- Who is responsible for implementing the communications strategy?
- Who will be working on the project?
- Who will be affected by the project?
- Who do we need to involve in the project process, e.g. in the steering group or the management group?
- Who will need to be consulted?
- Who do we need to inform?
- When do we need to communicate?
- What will you communicate?
- How will you communicate?
- What channels are required for feedback?
- Who is responsible for giving, receiving and acting on feedback?

Information and advice on the use of reports, presentations and websites in disseminating information about the project is given in Chapter 6. Information on the use of electronic communications – e-mail, social media, conference or chat rooms and videoconferencing – is considered in Chapters 6 and 7.

Risk analysis and management

At the very beginning of a project start thinking about what might go wrong. Risk analysis involves thinking about what might go wrong, resulting in a failed or delayed project. The end result of carrying out a risk analysis on a large or complex project can be a scary looking spreadsheet colour coded in green, red and orange. The actual risk assessment process is relatively simple and involves answering the following questions:

• What can go wrong?
• How likely is this to happen?
• What is the likely impact on the project if something goes wrong?
• How serious is each risk?
• How can the risks be managed?

Once you have asked these basic questions you can start a more detailed analysis of the risks:

1 What can go wrong?
2 How likely is this to happen?
   – *high probability* (> 80% likely to happen)
   – *medium probability* (20–80% likely to happen)
   – *low probability* (<20% likely to happen)
3 What is the likely impact on the project?
   – *high* – serious impact on project
   – *medium* – less serious impact on project
   – *low* – minimum effect on project and its outcomes
4 How serious is each risk? Identify the potential effect on the project by ranking risks using the answers to questions 2 and 3, as demonstrated in Table 3.5.
5 How can the risks be managed?
   – *high risks* – need to be taken into account in the project planning process, carefully considered at the start of the project, carefully monitored, and reviewed at each project management and steering group meeting as they could lead to the cancellation of the project; contingency plans must be created to help deal with these risks
   – *medium risks* – need to be carefully monitored and reviewed at each project meeting; if necessary advice and guidance on them would be sought at the steering group
   – *low risks* – need to be carefully monitored and reviewed at each project group and team meeting.

This risk analysis process is subjective and only as good as the estimates of the project team and manager. If you are involved in carrying out this type of process it's worth ensuring that your team includes people willing to take an optimistic and pessimistic perspective, as this will help you to carry out a balanced risk assessment.

Table 3.5 illustrates the likely impact of different levels of risk in a project and it indicates how different combinations of likelihood and impact may be scored.

Table 3.5 *Assessing the likely impact of different levels of risk on a project*

How likely is this to happen?	What is the likely impact on the project?		
	High	Medium	Low
High	XXX	XXX	XX
Medium	XXX	XXX	X
Low	XX	X	X

The items marked XXX are high risk and are treated as 'red'. They need to be carefully considered at the start of the project and could lead to the cancellation of the project. Contingency plans must be created to help deal with these risks. These risks need to be carefully monitored and reviewed at each project, management and steering group meeting.

The items marked XX are medium risk and are treated as 'orange'. These risks need to be carefully monitored and reviewed at each project group meeting. If necessary these medium risk issues would be escalated to the steering group for their advice and guidance.

The items marked X are low risk and are treated as 'green'. These risks need to be carefully monitored and reviewed at regular intervals.

A risk analysis for large and complex projects can cover up to 100 risks, where each risk is allocated a 'risk owner' who is responsible for monitoring the risk and then reporting to the steering group, project management group or the project team. The following case study describes a risk analysis made for a relatively simple and straightforward project: developing a new induction process in a college library.

Case study 3.5   Working out the risks for a project to develop a new library induction process in a law firm

Table 3.6 illustrates a risk analysis for a relatively small and simple project to develop a new library induction process in a law firm by two librarians, a graphic designer and a library assistant. The librarian led the project; the project team met each week. There was no need for a steering group or a project management group as it was a relatively small project. The law librarian reported directly to the business director who was responsible for student experience.

Table 3.6 *Assessing the risks for a project to develop a new induction process in a law library*

What are the potential risks?	How likely is this to happen? (High, medium or low)?	What is the likely impact on the project? (High, medium or low)?	How serious is each risk? (See Table 3.5 for guidance)	How can this risk be managed?
Key staff will take sick leave	Low	High	XX (orange)	Ensure everything is on shared drive; keep detailed notes from weekly project meetings
New resources won't be ready on time	Medium	Medium	XXX (red)	Monitor carefully; identify essential and nice to have elements in case need to revise project
Move of print room may affect ability to print materials on time	High	High	XXX (red)	Find out plans of print room staff; if necessary budget for outsourcing
Business director may require last minute changes to project	Low	High	XX (orange)	Keep director updated throughout project; ask for final amendments 4 weeks before induction resources go to print and is released online
Difficulty contacting new recruits via social media or e-mail	Medium	High	XXX (red)	Explain concerns to HR and ICT staff; ask about their back-up plans

Legal issues

Depending on the project, a number of legal issues may arise during the project work and it is worth thinking about these and obtaining appropriate advice if required at a very early stage in the life of the project. Typical legal areas to be taken into account are:

- employment law
- health and safety
- data protection
- copyright.

It is beyond the scope of this book to provide a summary of the relevant legislation (as it keeps changing) or to provide detailed advice on specific issues. The key advice is to contact relevant professionals at the very start of the project and identify any potential legal issues that should be considered during the life of the project.

Case study 3.6   Health and safety during a library move

I was the project manager for the move of an academic library into a new building. In addition to the permanent staff, 17 temporary 'movers and shifters' were employed to carry out much of the manual work. Just before the move began, the health and safety officer gave the permanent staff a refresher course on lifting and moving, and a half-day course on lifting and moving to the temporary staff on their first day of employment. These courses were carefully documented and everyone was expected to sign an attendance sheet at the start and end of the course. The course outline and all teaching materials were retained by the project team as part of their documentation process. All staff involved in the move were given appropriate safety clothes, e.g. high visibility jacket and safety boots.

On the second day of employment, one of the temporary staff damaged his foot and attempted to sue the university. After a long-drawn-out process managed by the university's solicitor, the case was dropped as the project manager and university were able to demonstrate that they had taken appropriate action to inform temporary and permanent staff about good practice in manual handling, which was well documented throughout the training course, and that the person in question had 'broken the rules'.

This was a very stressful process even though we were confident about winning the case and had carried out the project work in line with the recommendations of the health and safety office of the university.

Project documentation

It is important to think about how to document the project at an early stage as an effective documentation process will help support the project processes, and ensure you have all the information required throughout the life of the project and after it has closed. Think about questions such as:

- Who will be responsible for the project documentation?
- What documents will you need to support the work of the project team?
- What documents will you need to inform different groups of stakeholders?
- How will you record key decisions?
- Who will be responsible for ensuring the documentation is kept up to date?
- Who will have access to the documentation, e.g. via a shared drive?

A useful guiding question that will help develop a useful documentation system is to imagine that the project manager and team win the lottery and all resign from their posts. How will the project continue with a minimum of disruption? If you set up a system that will survive this (unlikely) scenario it will be robust.

Project finances

At the start of the project consider the project's finances. These are common costs in library and information service projects:

- people – permanent and contract staff
- external assistance – consultants, trainers
- furniture
- equipment
- software
- subscriptions
- consumables
- printed materials
- conference fees
- travel and subsistence.

Producing a project brief

As a result of informal discussions and initial research you can produce a project brief (or project overview statement), a short document (no more than two sides of A4) that outlines the proposed project and addresses the following questions:

• Why is the project important to the library and information service, and its parent institution?
• What is the overall aim or purpose of the project?
• What are the predicted project outcomes?
• What will it cost?
• Who will be involved in the project?
• When will it take place?
• What are the risks involved in the project?

The project brief serves a number of purposes:

• to focus the mind and start the process of moving from 'a good idea' to a project plan
• as a discussion document in meetings when trying to obtain a decision to approve the project
• as a briefing document at the first project meeting
• as a communication tool for other staff within the ILS and across the wider organisation
• as the basis of a range of other documents e.g. marketing, website information, annual report.

The written project brief is likely to be presented using the following types of headings:

• title of project
• aim of project
• main project outcomes
• benefits of completing the project
• rationale for project
• project stakeholders and how they will benefit from the project
• project milestones (key stages in the project process)
• resource requirements

- project communications strategy
- potential risks and how they may be managed
- proposed project management structure
- proposed project team
- relationship between this project and other projects.

The content of the project brief varies from project to project and organisation to organisation. Before starting to write one find out if your library and information service, or organisation has a standard template. Standard project management methodologies such as PRINCE2® or Agile provide guidance and templates on project documentation.

Obtaining the go-ahead

Once you have carried out the stages outlined in this chapter and developed the project brief the next step is to obtain approval to go ahead with the project. For small-scale projects this may be gained from a manager or director. In large-scale projects follow the normal approval processes of your library and information service, and organisation. This may entail presenting your proposal, perhaps using standard templates, to one or more committees or boards. Be prepared to present your project idea formally, e.g. in a 15 minute presentation, and talk through and defend the project brief. If you need to gain approval for a large project it is worth speaking to the key decision-makers informally before they attend the decision-making meeting(s) as this should help you to convince them that your project needs their support.

When bidding for funding for a project there is a two-stage process: gaining approval from your organisation and then from the funding body following the formal submission of a competitive bid or tender (see Chapter 8).

Whatever the process, it is important to gain approval for a new project, ideally in writing or by e-mail, before you start the detailed planning. Otherwise you may waste a lot of time and effort in detailed planning if approval is not given for the project. The next chapter outlines the project-planning process.

Summary

This chapter described the work that needs to take place at the very start of the project: thinking about the key characteristics of the project (e.g.

aims and outcomes, scope), the people involved in the project work and as stakeholders, risk analysis, legal issues and finance. The main output from this work is a project brief, which is used to obtain approval for the project to go ahead. Once approval has been gained for the project you move into the detailed planning stage, when you revisit many of the themes covered in this chapter and consider them in much more detail.

References

Caperon, L. (2015) Developing Adaptable, Efficient Mobile Library Services: librarians as enablers, *Ariadne*, **73**, www.ariadne.ac.uk/issue73/caperon.

Coffin, A. and Morrill, S. (2015) Promoting Innovation: the WiLS model, *Collaborative Librarianship*, **7** (1), Article 6, http://digitalcommons.du.edu/cgi/.

Demco Interiors for Designing Libraries (2012) *Managing a Successful Library Design and Furnishing Project*, www.designinglibraries.org.uk/.

King, N. (2013) Project Management for Assessment: a case study, *Library Leadership and Management*, **27** (1–2), 1–9.

Rogers, E. M. (1983) *Diffusion of Innovations*, 3rd edn, Free Press of Glencoe.

CHAPTER 4

Planning the project

Introduction

This chapter introduces the planning process and highlights the importance of detailed planning to successful project management. Project planning involves repeating some of the activities carried out at the previous stage in the project process, which resulted in the production of the project brief (Chapter 3). At the planning stage it is necessary to go into much more detail and work out the nuts and bolts of the project.

Small projects require an action plan with an associated plan to resource the project (people and finances) and undertake a risk analysis. Pull together this information with the original project brief (see Chapter 3) to create a project plan, which should provide sufficient information to gain approval for the plan and for the project to go ahead.

In large and complex projects Gantt charts and PERT diagrams (or equivalent tools) are required when creating a project plan, with the subsequent identification of the critical path (or their equivalent). The detail of the schedule helps you to calculate the workload of staff involved in the project and makes it possible to work out the detail of the project's documentation and communication processes and finances. The detailed plan can be pulled together as a report for the project sponsor to approve.

Researching the project

When researching the project external and internal analyses of the project environment are required.

External analysis

These are some questions to ask when carrying out an external analysis of the project environment:

- What political, economic or social factors may have an impact on the project?
- What is the current practice within the library and information profession towards the project?
- What is the current practice within the sector, e.g. government, health, education, voluntary sector, towards the project?
- Who has been involved in this type of project? Can you contact them and ask for lessons learnt from their experiences?
- Is it possible to visit library and information services that have implemented this type of project and learn from their experiences?

Internal analysis

These are some questions to ask when carrying out an internal analysis of the project environment:

- What is currently happening within my organisation, e.g. major projects or change management initiatives, which may have an impact on the project?
- What is happening within the different departments in my organisation that may have an impact (positively or negatively) on the project?
- Who are the likely champions of the project?
- Who is likely to block the project?
- What systems and procedures within the organisation do I need to take into account when planning and implementing the project?

Developing the project infrastructure

Project managers identify the project infrastructure which will help support their project (see Chapter 3). For small-scale projects there will be a project team and the team leader will report to her manager or director. Large-scale and complex projects require a formal structure, which is likely to involve three groups: a steering group, a management group, and the project team. At this stage identify members of the project team, and for large-scale projects identify members of the three groups. Think about who will:

- contribute seniority and credibility
- provide access to resources, e.g. finance, space

- provide political and cultural know how and connections
- provide expertise, e.g. finance, human resource management
- act as gatekeeper – opening doors and helping to unblock issues
- represent different stakeholder groups
- carry out the project work.

Take time and advice before you finalise membership and send out invitations. If a key individual is missed off the original invitation list it could sour relations with that person for some time.

Producing and agreeing a schedule

A key task for any project manager is to develop the project schedule, which is a crucial document and provides the blue print for the project. The schedule outlines all the tasks that need to be completed and the time frame, and it includes who will carry out the work. The starting point for developing the schedule is the project brief, so it is worth re-reading it and being very clear about the project aims and outcomes.

Developing a schedule for a small-scale project is a relatively simple task and can be completed using brainstorming techniques and a spreadsheet (see Chapters 2 and 7). The best starting point when working out the schedule for a large-scale project, so it does not seem too overwhelming, is to break it into stages and tasks, as illustrated in Figure 4.1. Each project is

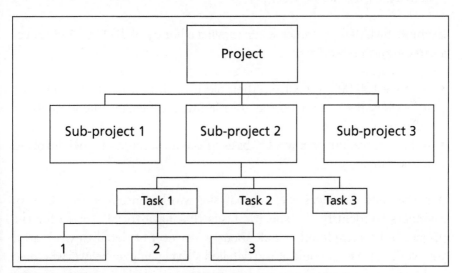

Figure 4.1 *The overall structure of a project*

divided into a series of sub-projects (which may be carried out at the same time) and each stage is divided into a series of tasks. Each task is then divided into a series of activities.

Analysing the tasks

Analyse the work content of all types of project by listing:

- tasks with specific outcomes
- recurrent tasks
- milestones.

The specific outcomes of the project are best identified as SMART (specific, measurable, achievable, realistic and timebound). These objectives are:

- *specific* – describe a particular activity
- *measurable* – can be measured or identified when complete as there will be something tangible to see or hear
- *achievable* – can be achieved; you are not being asked to achieve an impossible task, e.g. one that involves a new invention
- *realistic* – can be achieved with the resources available and in the time required
- *timebound* – have a deadline or set amount of time given to the activity, e.g. an hour a week.

Example SMART outcomes when moving a library of 100,000 items over a three-month period are:

- to move 100,000 items from their old to their new location and to have every book in the correct location with catalogue amendments by 1 September 2018
- to inform readers on a weekly basis of the movement of stock involved in the move.

A simple and practical way of analysing work content is to ask team members to identify the specific tasks that have to take place for the project to be completed. Think about what level of detail to work at: if you work out the schedule at too detailed a level you may be overwhelmed with tasks; conversely if you produce very general tasks you may miss out key areas that will need attention. The following case studies give some indication of the levels of detail used in different projects.

Case study 4.1   Developing a student learning resource on plagiarism

A college librarian working with the study skills tutor decided to establish an online learning resource on plagiarism aimed at students taking a range of courses in the health and social care department. They identified the following tasks:

- Produce sample questions and answers.
- Load questions into learning environment.
- Pilot sample questions (and answers).

They spent some time converting these outline tasks into SMART ones, and the initial list was as follows:

- Produce project brief and obtain approval for the project.
- Inform tutors of project and ask for their involvement via e-mail.
- Produce 20 sample questions and answers.
- Load questions into learning environment.
- Ask four colleagues to pilot questions and answers.
- Edit questions and answers in response to feedback.
- Load final version into the VLE.
- Launch initiative to colleagues and students.

This list had to be converted into a set of SMART deadlines by adding a deadline for each task. The librarian achieved this by working backwards from the start of term and the project launch, and then identifying the start and end date for each of these activities. This information was used to produce a project plan using project management software as discussed in Chapter 7. By using the project management software, the librarian and study skills tutor were able to check their project plan and the Gantt chart, check the timeline for the project, and know who was assigned to each task (see Chapter 7, figures 7.3, 7.4 and 7.5). This process of converting the outline tasks into SMART tasks enabled them to identify additional tasks that had to be carried out and have a very clear picture of the work necessary before the start of the new academic year.

Recurrent tasks

In addition to the specific tasks required to complete the project remember to consider the recurrent tasks repeated at regular intervals throughout the project, for example:

- holding regular project team meetings
- sending out a weekly project news bulletin
- updating the project spreadsheet
- updating the risk register.

These recurrent tasks are sometimes omitted at the project scheduling stage, which results in a serious underestimate of the amount of time that will be spent on the project.

Milestones

At this stage in the scheduling process, it is also worth thinking about and identifying milestones – significant landmarks in the life of a project. A milestone is not a task or an activity but a sign that a stage has been completed in the project. Examples of milestones include project start, project end, end of Phase 1, completion of staff training, and completion of installation of new hardware and software. Milestones provide important markers to the project manager and team as they may be used to signal to the stakeholders that the project is on course. Milestones can also be motivators for the project workers as they show them that their work has outcomes.

Estimating duration

Estimate how long each task takes. If you are completely new to the type of tasks included in your project schedule ask an experienced colleague (from your own or another library service) for help.

Recording your work

One approach to capturing all this information is to write the name of each task on a sticky note (see Figure 4.2). Give each task a number (starting with 1) as this will come in useful at a later stage. Different coloured sticky notes may be used to indicate the main tasks, recurrent tasks and milestones. I have used this technique in the initial scheduling meetings of library and information service projects and found that colleagues enjoy using it and a whole range of tasks are identified very quickly.

Example format for recording details of tasks on a sticky note		
Task number	Name of task	Estimated duration
Earliest start date		Latest start date

Example format of a completed sticky note

Task number 3	Produce 20 sample questions and answers	Estimated duration: 1 day
Earliest start date: 21-7-2018		Latest start date: 30-7-2018

Figure 4.2 *Example format of a sticky note used to record details of a task, and example of a completed sticky note*

Estimating staff hours to carry out a task

At a later stage in the project scheduling process you have to estimate the number of staff hours or days that someone will have to spend carrying out a task. It is worth highlighting the difference between these two time measurements:

- the duration is the amount of time that a task will take, normally measured in days, weeks or months
- the staff time or effort is the amount of time individuals will spend working on that task, e.g. two people for eight hours each, or four people for four hours each.

Working out the logical sequence of events.

The next step is to work out the order of tasks by showing the relationships or dependencies between the different tasks using this logic:

- *Finish to start* – Task B can start when Task A is complete.
- *Start to start* – Task B can start at the same time as Task C.

- *Finish to finish* – Task C must finish when Task B finishes.
- *Start to finish* – when Task B starts Task C must finish.

The finish-to-start relationship is the most common one that project managers deal with, where B cannot take place until A is completed (Figure 4.3).

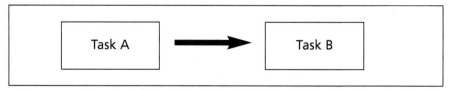

Figure 4.3 *The finish-to-start relationship*

If you are developing the project plan using sticky notes then the logic can be added by laying out all the sticky notes on a large piece of paper or whiteboard, and drawing in arrows to show the relationships between the tasks. If you are using project management software this result is achieved by linking tasks using task numbers. Whichever method you use, the end result is a logic diagram.

Remember to include milestones, all project schedules have at least two – start and end. Some tasks take place sequentially (Figure 4.4); others take place concurrently (Figure 4.5).

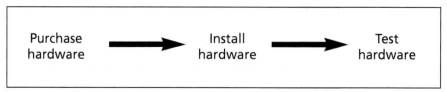

Figure 4.4 *Example of sequential tasks*

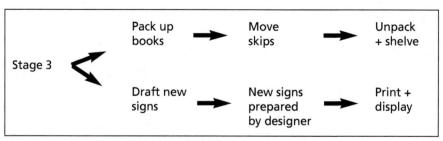

Figure 4.5 *Example of concurrent tasks*

Working out the critical path
The critical path of a project links the critical tasks – those tasks which if they are not completed on time result in the project not meeting its deadline. The critical path is illustrated in Figure 4.6 where tasks A, B, C and E each take five days to complete. Task D takes one day to complete. The whole project from Task A to Task E takes 20 days to complete. If the time taken to complete tasks A, B, C or E slips the whole project timetable will slip and the project will take longer than expected. Therefore tasks A, B, C and E are critical as indicated by their darker shading and the pathway that connects them is the critical path (if you are using project management software the critical path is normally illustrated in red). In contrast, if Task D takes between 1 and 10 days to complete the project will still be on time (as it will take ten days to complete tasks B and C).

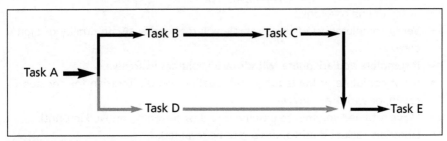

Figure 4.6 *Example of a critical path*

One method of working out the critical path is to identify the start and end dates for the project, then work through the tasks from beginning to end and list the earliest start and finish dates for each task. Write these dates on the relevant sticky note (see Figure 4.2). Then work through the tasks noting the latest start and finish dates for each task. Again, note them on the relevant sticky note. The critical path is the set of activities where the earliest and latest finish dates are the same; their timing is crucial if the project is to remain on schedule. Any time slippage across the critical path has a major impact on the project.

In some project management software packages the critical path is automatically worked out; it is often displayed in red on the screen. This is useful information, as once you know which tasks form the critical path you will know where to put in additional effort if the project deadlines begin to slip.

Working out the workflow and process for a particular task

After working out the tasks and timeline of the project, the workflow within a particular task – the process for carrying out a specific task and detailed criteria for making decisions – must be identified. This is illustrated in the following case study.

Case study 4.2   A weeding project

Thomas and Shouse (2012) describe a large-scale weeding (deselection) project, introduced to make space for a new campus partner at the East Carolina University Joyner Library. They identify the workflow for package-based weeding as follows:

- Examine licence for post-cancellation rights.
- Search title lists for print holdings.
- Verify online coverage.
- Verify completeness of three sample volumes and evaluate quality of digital copy.
- If complete and adequate, withdraw all volumes in archive.
- If not complete or inadequate scan quality, consult librarian for decision to retain, or withdraw anyway.
- Move retained volumes to basement (unless currently received in print).
- Librarian decides if microfilms are to be retained.

They also describe the rules used to make decisions about the stock:

- withdraw:
  - bound volumes in archival packages
  - dead runs or incomplete runs no longer received in print, especially if the last volume is 1999 or earlier; there are fewer than ten volumes; they are not indexed; journals are no longer relevant for university curricula
- send to storage:
  - long runs of titles no longer received in print, especially if online access is available (from any provider), they have subject area importance or there is another local reason to retain them
  - poorly scanned or leftover volumes from titles in archival package (if greater than ten) if accessible online
- keep in stacks:
  - current print subscriptions
  - recent long runs (of 30 volumes or more) with no electronic access
  - items of subject area importance
  - items of significant value to local collections.

Thomas and Shouse (2012) describe how these rules of thumb helped them to achieve their goal of making more space within the library and provided a way forward to manage the print collection effectively. Articles such as this provide useful detail on the project workflow and decision-making activities for anyone involved in a weeding project. They can be adapted to suit the context of a specific library or information service.

Staffing the project

At the planning stage of the project think about the people side of the work and how you will be able to staff the project:

- Who will be carrying out the work?
- Will you be working with permanent staff or contract staff?
- What specialist knowledge or skills do they require?
- How much time will it take them to carry out their project work?

Think about how much time each person will have to spend on the project. Are they going to have enough time to complete their project work? How will this fit into their everyday workload?

When you allocate tasks within a team, the work may be shared out according to personal interests, job role, experience or expertise, available time or personal development needs. Individuals may volunteer for particular tasks or activities, or may be asked if they would like to take responsibility for particular tasks. It is important to identify constructive solutions when there are difficulties in agreeing responsibilities. If the team cannot agree responsibilities it may be worth noting preferences, conflicts of preference and constructive solutions.

When library and information workers are assigned to a project their assignation is often temporary and the project work may run alongside their main job role. Carroll (2000) advises that if project workers are spending less than 50% of their time on their project work they may have difficulty in prioritising the project work over their other work. In reality many library and information workers spend less than 50% of their time on project work so need to be effective time managers if they are to complete their project work. This issue is considered in more depth in Chapter 1.

It is useful to estimate the amount of staff time required for a project. You can do this for a complex project using a simple equation (found in most standard project management books). First give pessimistic, average and optimistic estimates of the time it will take to complete a task. Then use this equation to work out the amount of staff time you need:

$$\text{time (estimated)} = \frac{\text{time (pessimistic)} + 4 \times \text{time (average)} + \text{time (optimistic)}}{6}$$

Case study 4.3   Developing an online resource: estimating staff time

A community college is developing an online study skills resource. The project manager is estimating the time it will take one person to upload ten online quizzes onto the college's VLE. She estimates the following times:

- most pessimistic time = 12 hours
- average time = 5 hours
- most optimistic time = 3 hours.

What is the likely time this activity will take?

$$\text{time (likely)} = \{12 + (4 \times 5) + 3\} \div 6$$

The answer is approximately 5.8 hours

At the planning stage, using this estimate, the project manager rounded the figure up and input 6 hours for the completion of this task into the project plan. Once the project was implemented, she found that the actual task took 3 hours to complete. This difference in time between the planned and the actual time caused no problems at all. However, if the task had taken 12 hours and the project plan had included an estimate of only 6 hours it may have caused some problems.

One of the practical dangers of using this type of equation is that it can give the impression of accuracy. In fact the estimate is only as good as the assessment of the optimistic, pessimistic and average times used in the equation. In practice, project managers and teams can improve the accuracy of this process by:

- asking a range of staff for an input into the estimates
- measuring the amount of time it actually takes someone to complete the task
- contacting professional colleagues who have been involved in similar tasks and asking them for their estimates.

It is also necessary to work out how many days per month (or year) that someone is able to work on the project by identifying the number of days they work per year and subtracting days for training, weekends, annual leave, statutory days and sick days as follows:

Working days = Days in year − (annual leave + weekends + training
per year   + statutory days + sick days)
             = 365 − (20 + 104 + 4 + 11 + 5) days
             = 221 days per annum

So as a rough rule of thumb, someone who is working on a project full time will be available for approximately 221 days' work per year and someone who is spending 50% of their work time on the project will be available for 115.5 days per year. It is important to allocate people on the basis of their actual working days per year otherwise you will seriously underestimate the staffing input required for the project.

Presenting a detailed plan

You will need to present your detailed plan for discussion and approval to the project team, management group and (possibly) the steering committee. There are three main methods of presenting the project plan:

- using action plans
- using Gantt charts
- using PERT diagrams.

Action plans

In simple projects the whole project plan can be illustrated with an action plan that shows who does what and the timescale (see Figure 4.7).

Task	Person responsible	Start date	End date
Book conference facilities	Jane	6 January	15 January
Book speakers	Chris	16 January	31 January
Produce publicity materials	Sam	1 February	28 February
Send out mail shot	Sam	1 March	31 March

Figure 4.7 *Example of an action plan*

Gantt charts

Gantt charts are used to show the project tasks that take place within a particular time period, for example a week or month. The technical name for the charts comes from their developer Henry Gantt (1861–1919). If you are working on a small project or don't have access to project manager software you can produce the bar or Gantt charts using a whiteboard and pens, a wall calendar and sticky paper, or a spreadsheet. An example Gantt chart is shown in Figure 4.8.

Many project managers and teams use Gantt charts because they are easy to read, show the relationship between the project tasks and the timescale of the project, and recurrent (or repeated) tasks and milestones. It is very easy to look at a Gantt chart and identify times when there may be pressure on the project, for example as a result of information workers' holidays or peaks in customer demands. However, they have two main disadvantages: they don't show the relationships between different tasks and they don't show the critical path.

Figure 4.8 presents a basic Gantt chart, which shows the tasks that need to be carried out for organising a conference and their timescale. This type of Gantt chart can be prepared using the table function in basic word processing software or a spreadsheet. Alternatively, if you use project management software then inputting this type of data may also result in the production of a PERT (or similar) diagram without any additional input of data.

Case study 4.4   Early stages of organising a conference

Tasks	January	February	March	April	May
Book conference facilities	■				
Book speakers		■			
Produce publicity materials			■		
Send out mail shot				■	
Manage bookings					■
Run conference					■

Figure 4.8 *Example of a Gantt chart*

PERT diagrams

Another way of obtaining a clear picture and detailed information about the project is to produce a PERT (programme evaluation and review technique) diagram; this type of diagram was developed in the USA. A PERT diagram shows the logical relationship between tasks, which may be prepared using a large piece of paper and pen, a whiteboard or project management software. PERT diagrams are very similar to flowcharts and provide an overview or the 'big picture' of the project. Their advantage over Gantt charts is that they show the relationships between the tasks. PERT diagrams produced electronically often have the critical path highlighted in red, which makes it very easy for the project manager to identify those tasks which must be completed on time if the whole project is to meet its deadline. However PERT diagrams can be large and difficult to work from. If you use project management software it can be very difficult to see the whole view of the project on a single screen. Example PERT diagrams are shown in figures 4.9 and 4.10. The example in Figure 4.10 was produced using SmartDraw®.

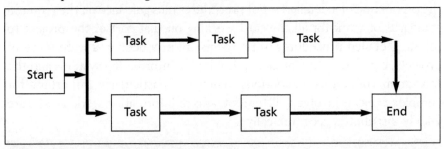

Figure 4.9 *Example of a PERT diagram*

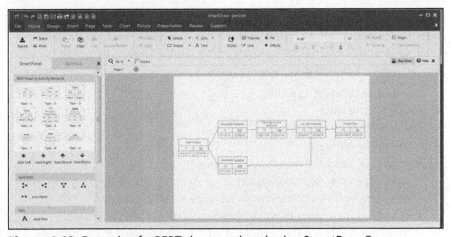

Figure 4.10 *Example of a PERT chart produced using SmartDraw®*
Source: SmartDraw (www.smartdraw.com)

Communicating a plan

It is important to think about the way in which you will communicate your project plan. In my experience, action plans and Gantt charts are the most commonly used methods as they are easy to read and work through. In contrast, PERT diagrams, particularly for large and complex projects, can be difficult to present and work through in a meeting and are perhaps best kept for use by the project manager and team. Many project management software packages enable you to export files and images from your project plan into everyday office packages such as Word and PowerPoint, which enables you to provide good quality images to support your communications.

How will the tasks be carried out?

In the previous sections, the project schedule identifies the what, who and when of the project. An important aspect of project management is thinking about how the work will be carried out. This is likely to result in the production of a detailed set of procedures plus guidance on the required standards of work for all the staff working on that part of the project to follow. Detailed procedures or protocols are produced in a wide range of projects, e.g. digitisation projects, developing information systems and the movement of library collections. They are particularly important for complex projects involving different teams of information workers who are widely distributed geographically.

Case study 4.5   Moving a library

This case study describes some of the activities at Dublin City Library where staff were involved in moving a library and reorganising its collection at the same time. Allen and Bowden (2001) provide a very detailed description of the process, which included the following tasks:

- an initial stock weeding project
- measuring the stock
- designing the new library layout
- calculating shelf space
- re-organising stock for new spaces, including:
  - thinking about the visual impact
  - re-arranging some collections to enhance visual impact
  - allocating shelf space using photocopies of new building and stock measurement figures, marking out each collection by using a different colour

- devising a transfer coding system with a colour–number–letter sequence
- labelling shelves in the old library using a colour-coded A4 card attached to shelves written in duplicate (for the old and the new library), showing the shelf number, collection details and subject floor
- labelling individual shelves in the old library using coloured, easy-peel, self-adhesive labels attached to the crates
- keeping an inventory of all shelf numbers
- marking plans to ensure that the materials were correctly shelved
- labelling shelves in the new library
- developing working practices with the moving company.

Allen and Bowden (2001) describe how numbers of library staff working at different times on the project may change to match the specific tasks taking place, so it is necessary to work out carefully what is required with the moving company, e.g. who is responsible for each aspect of the physical move down to the level of putting labels on the crates.

Working out the finances
When planning the project the finances need to be worked out. This is described in Chapter 8.

Carrying out a detailed risk analysis
Risk analyses were introduced in Chapter 3, which included a simple methodology for carrying one out. As you approach the end of the planning process it is worth performing it again as you will now have a more detailed understanding of the project and what it entails. The results of the risk analysis should be included in the project plan.

Designing the project evaluation process
At the project planning stage think about and start to develop the evaluation process so you can collect the relevant information during the project implementation process. Further information about project evaluation is presented in Chapter 6.

Documenting the project
At the planning stage think about how you will record and document the project. In all projects, it is worth considering making all project document-ation available on a shared drive. Clearly you will need to document:

- all project meetings and reports
- key stages: project brief, project plan, records of project implementation process, project evaluation report
- key e-mails, e.g. confirming project approval and budget
- consultation activities and feedback from stakeholders.

A simple and very useful document is a work diary in which key project activities and decisions are recorded. These are particularly valuable for long-term projects lasting one or more years, when there is a need to recall something that occurred earlier in the life of the project.

There are different ways to keep a project work diary which may be kept by the project manager and/or team leaders (in large projects) and/or team members.

Reporting progress

At the initial planning stages it is important to think about how the project manager will obtain information about the project's progress. This process will be refined in more detail after the production of the detailed project plan. In general, the project manager needs to obtain information about the progress of the project, for example from team workers, to identify feedback:

- on the progress of the project plan – significant dates and milestones, significant constraints, potential and existing problems, and creep or slack in project time
- from users and other stakeholders
- from library and information colleagues.

The project manager reports progress to her manager and the following groups (as appropriate):

- the project steering group
- the project management team
- the funding organisation
- library and information service colleagues and customers
- stakeholders
- senior managers.

The type of reports used to keep everyone informed depends on the project and all the different stakeholders. Common reports include management reports, milestone reports and financial reports. The structure of the reports can vary from informal to extremely formal. Externally funded projects generally have very strict rules about reporting and specify the reporting process, including the form and report templates (see Chapter 8). It is worth spending some time at the start of the project to identify the reporting requirements so you can set up the appropriate systems to provide the necessary information for the reports. This will ensure that the reporting process is well managed and does not involve last-minute panics as the project manager and team discover they have not collected the correct information.

At the end of the project, the project manager often writes formal reports, for example a final summary report and a final financial report, which may include an internal project evaluation and review reports. Many projects are also reviewed by an external agency, which results in an external project evaluation and review form to be completed. Again, it is worth thinking about the final project reports at the start of the project process so you can plan for their production throughout the project process. This topic is covered in Chapter 6.

Developing a project communication strategy and plan
At the planning stage of the project, think about your communication strategy and how you will communicate with two main groups: the project team(s) and the external stakeholders – customers, colleagues not involved in the project, and the library and information profession.

Communications within the team
Internal communications within the project team are likely to take place via meetings, e-mails, phone calls and a website. The project manager and team decide on their working practices, considering factors such as:

- use of a shared drive
- use of a whiteboard within the office
- use of e-mail and practices with regards to copying and blind copying e-mails
- use of project management and/or collaborative software (see Chapter 7)

- normal response times to colleagues' e-mails
- how to deal with absences (holidays or sickness).

Communications beyond the project team

The project manager and team communicate their work to stakeholders beyond the project team through an external information and communication process, which is a vital part of the project. Ideally stakeholders should be kept informed about the project from start to finish so they don't receive any unexpected shocks or surprises, though it is important not to over-communicate and cause boredom or information overload.

The amount of time and energy devoted to the external communications depends on the nature of the project. In major projects the project team may have a working party whose primary consideration is the external communication process. Developing a strategy helps to ensure that all aspects of external communications are considered in some detail:

- What is the purpose of the external communication strategy?
- Who is responsible for implementing the external communications strategy?
- With whom will you communicate?
- What will you communicate?
- How you will communicate – through e-mail, website, social media, weekly update, leaflets and posters, briefing meetings?
- How will you obtain feedback about the project and its impact?
- Who is responsible for giving, receiving and acting on feedback?

It is worth working through these questions with the project team and using your answers to develop an external communication strategy. In general, use as many different forms of communication as possible – meetings, presentations, workshops, briefings, press releases, e-mails, social media, newsletters, posters and reports – and repeat your message a number of times.

Future-proofing a project

If you are planning a project it is worth thinking about the future. What will happen to the project if you or other key team members leave before it is completed? Will the project be sustainable? Farkas (2015), a faculty librarian in a community college in the USA, writes about the importance of future proofing your project:

Whenever I leave a job, I worry about projects I led or supported. When you put months or years into something you feel passionately about, it can start to feel like your baby. When you leave for a new position, you have to put that baby's future into someone else's hands. Developing a sense of detachment can be difficult. It is easier to leave a project behind when you know there are people equipped and committed to supporting it. I've heard horror stories about libraries that have not been able to maintain technologies – from blogs and Facebook pages to mission-critical, homegrown software after an employee left. It's challenging to think of leaving as part of project planning…

Here is a summary of the advice Farkas (2015) provides to make sure your project is sustainable if you or colleagues leave:

- Make sure your project is aligned with the library strategy.
- Think about how easy it will be to maintain the technology. Do you have the staff capacity to maintain it? If you are using subscription-based software is there funding to maintain it?
- Who will maintain the project in the future?
- Is your documentation thorough and up to date?
- How will you assess and evaluate the project?

Bringing it all together

The output of the planning stage is a project plan, which will be used as a formal working document by project workers. There are a number of methods of producing this plan. In very large and complex projects the project plan may be written up in the form of a detailed specification identifying the detail of the project process, the resource requirements and the boundaries of the project. In small and relatively simple projects the project manager and team can produce a simple plan. These types of project plans are outlined below.

Small-scale and simple project plans

In relatively small-scale and simple projects there is no need to produce sophisticated project plans. It is often sufficient to produce a project plan that contains:

- a project brief

- an action plan
- details of staffing implications
- details of financial requirements
- a risk analysis.

Large-scale and complex project plans

Large and complex projects, particularly those involving different units, departments or organisations, require a project specification as a tool for deciding and confirming the boundaries and details of the project, and the responsibilities of key staff. It is an important document and once agreed lays down the project parameters. Any changes to the project require the re-negotiation of the project specification.

The specification can be a valuable tool for the project manager, if only because it can be used to prevent stakeholders (including senior managers and directors) from moving the goalposts and changing the project outcomes or resources without discussions and/or the agreement of the project manager and management team. Different organisations have their own standard project specification template but the structure of a project specification is typically as follows:

- title page
- introduction
- purpose
- background
- goals and objectives
- scope and limitations
- strategy
- description of main activities
- project schedule
- resources
- finance
- list of staff and their involvement
- connections to other activities
- transitional arrangements
- communication strategy
- management structure
- reporting schedule
- risks

- quality standards, processes and procedures
- intellectual property, patents and licences
- insurance
- distribution list
- formal approval (signature, name, date).

The contents of project specifications vary depending on the project and they may be called by other names such as project definition, plan or strategy.

Case study 4.6   A collaborative approach to develop a new library system

Saarti et al. (2015) describe the aim of a project to assess the feasibility of introducing a comprehensive library system for all types of libraries in Finland. Libraries from different library sectors in Finland have different traditions, domains of expertise, and social environment. The project plan included:

- discussion of joint guidelines and culture (e.g. principles for lending and cataloguing)
- information on products and functions based on library systems
- information on the opportunities and needs of joint databases (bibliographic, collections, customer and similar databases)
- joint and tailored sections
- information on standards and interfaces
- a risk analysis
- a financing solution and cost-benefit analysis
- an administrative model and a discussion of legal issues
- a timetable.

Communicating the project plan

If the project team produced the plan collaboratively they are likely to feel ownership over it, but if the project manager produced the plan alone it should be circulated and promoted to the relevant people: the project team, the management team and, if appropriate, the steering group.

It may be helpful to break down very detailed project specifications and only present different audiences with the particular section that is relevant to them, as described in this case study.

> **Case study 4.7   Preventing information overload**
>
> I worked with a university's estate staff on a project to close the university's learning resource centre and move its contents to three locations. At my first meeting with the estate operations manager I handed him a copy of the project plan (88 pages of A4). A look of horror crossed his face. I quickly realised that my detailed plan had resulted in information overload and agreed to send him a one-page overview and weekly summaries of what needed to be moved where each week. It was a salutary lesson in communication skills!

Gaining approval for the project plan

In many projects, the approval to go ahead is made on the basis of the project plan. This makes the project plan a crucial document. Once you have gained approval for your project, e.g. from your line manager or the steering group, you can move on to the next stage: project implementation.

Summary

This chapter gave an overview of the project planning process and included case studies and examples that are relevant to small-scale, simple, large-scale or complex projects. There is an extensive range of project management tools and techniques, e.g. Gantt charts, PERT diagrams, and calculation of the critical path, that are helpful in working out the project plan. Project management software is considered in Chapter 7. In general, it is vital to the success of the project to plan it at the level of detail that is appropriate for its success. Time spent on planning is rarely wasted and it may help you avoid making mistakes.

Project planning involves working with a wide range of people and it is necessary to consider their roles in the project and your communication strategy. The people side of projects is vital to their success. Chapters 9 and 10 discuss this in more detail. The next chapter focuses on implementing the project plan.

References

Allen, J. and Bowden, L. (2001) Move Over: moving DCU library's print material to the new library building, *SCONUL Newsletter*, **24**, 13–16, www.sconul.ac.uk.
Carroll, J. (2000) *Project 2000 in Easysteps*, Computer Step.
Farkas, M. (2015) Future-Proof Your Project: ensuring your work survives your

exit, *American Libraries*, **46** (6),
https://americanlibrariesmagazine.org/2015/06/15/future-proof-your-project/.

Saarti, J., Luokkanen, S., Ahlqvist, A. and Lager, L. (2015) Towards a New Library System: a paradigmatic shift in the Finnish library system planning and acquisition, *Library Management*, **36** (1/2), 2–11.

Thomas, W. J. and Shouse, D. L. (2012) Rules of Thumb for Deselecting, Relocating, and Retaining Bound Journals, *Collection Building*, **31** (3), 92–7.

CHAPTER 5

Implementation

Introduction

Once the project has been planned and approved, the implementation process starts and the project manager and team put the plan into action. This chapter considers the following topics: implementing the project by managing people and resources; rolling out the project plan; reporting on the project's progress; identifying and managing problems and potential problems, including blockages, project slippage, quality and complex issues; reviewing the project process; and completing the project.

Implementing the project plan

At the implementation stage of the project, the plan is put into action. This phase involves managing people, resources (e.g. finances) and the project process.

It is vital to the success of a project that the project team develops to become effective and focused by developing appropriate working practices. The team may be diverse and perhaps virtual, or made up of volunteers. If you are involved in working on a strategic project, you also need to consider the people side in some depth and use change management tools and techniques. Failure to take into account customers', colleagues', team members', partners' and/or stakeholders' responses to the project may lead to its collapse. Chapter 9 covers the people side of projects in detail and Chapter 10 discusses the process of working with partners.

Another important area for the project manager to manage is the finances. Basic knowledge about simple financial procedures of your organisation or funding body (if the project is externally funded) are essential if the project finances are to be professionally managed and kept within the project budget. Breaking basic financial rules may have serious consequences so gain advice and guidance from your organisation and the funding body (if the project is externally funded) before proceeding to implement the project. Financial management is considered in Chapter 8.

This section focuses on the project process: communications with the team, monitoring, tracking and – where necessary – taking corrective action. Effective project managers juggle many different tasks and issues, and respond proactively to problems and challenges as they arise during the project implementation process.

Keep in contact with the project team which is easiest if you are working in a shared office but even then there may be periods when you don't see each other. At the project planning stage, you will have established a team's communication protocol – for example daily or weekly updates, e.g. via e-mails or messaging – and stick to it. This may be achieved using project management software, which provides an e-mail or messaging function, or collaborative software (see Chapter 7 for information about the use of ICT to support the project implementation process).

Despite having prepared a detailed project plan, it is unlikely that everything will go exactly as anticipated. Your risk analysis will have identified potential trouble spots, which all need careful monitoring, and unforeseen situations may arise. A diverse range of factors can have adverse effects, for example:

- staff sickness
- delays in project team recruitment
- delays in the procurement process
- inaccurate estimations of the amount of time it will take to complete a task
- changes in the price of essential supplies
- failure to get permission to go ahead with a particular aspect of the project
- change in requirements by funding organisation or sponsor
- change in senior management resulting in a change in direction or resources
- unexpected events, e.g. fire, flood, landslide.

Project managers need to monitor the progress of the project. In particular, I always find it useful to keep an eye on the motivation and team working of the people involved in the project. Other key areas to monitor are tasks on the critical path, milestones, the budget and project communications.

There are a number of approaches to monitoring a project. In small-scale projects, it is a simple process to keep in touch with the team (if there is one) and to check on the action plan and whether or not you are achieving the SMART actions by the specified deadline. If you are working in a small team you can monitor and review the project progress at your regular team meetings and decide on any required changes or interventions.

In a large-scale project, follow a structured approach to monitoring its progress. Project managers who lead a number of teams can request that each team leader provides a formal report at regular intervals, e.g. weekly. Similarly, team leaders can request that their team workers each provide a formal report weekly (or even daily). These formal reports are then pulled together and summarised to provide weekly or monthly reports to the project management group and (as appropriate) to the steering group. In addition to the formal reports, it is useful to monitor the project through observation and informal discussions by walking about and talking to people, observing what is happening, and asking for mini-reports by e-mail when appropriate. One of the advantages of this approach is that sometimes small or potential problems, not recognised in the project plan, can be identified extremely early in the project process and a solution can be worked out with the team in question. It is beneficial to be curious and to constantly ask questions and keep an eye on all aspects of the project's progress.

In projects involving different people possibly working on different sites a simple process such as everyone e-mailing or texting the project manager (or posting the information on the project site) with information about the state of all the tasks at set times each week will keep the manager up to date. A simple structure for weekly feedback reports is presented in Figure 5.1 on the next page.

Standard project methodologies, e.g. PRINCE2® or Agile, provide a set of tools and templates for tracking the progress of a project, and project management software such as MS Project (see Chapter 7) helps in monitoring and reporting. It is relatively simple to obtain reports such as Gantt charts on completed, part-completed or non-started tasks, daily or weekly task lists, and individual task lists. However, this information is only reliable if it is up to date and accurate. If you are managing a complex project and set up systems to keep you informed of the status of individual tasks it is worth checking that the work has occurred, particularly if you are working with people you don't know very well, e.g. contractors. This is illustrated in the following case study.

Weekly progress report from:			
Task number	Start date	End date	Current status & comments
Major concerns and issues			
Signature		Date	

Figure 5.1 *Example of a weekly progress report form*

Case study 5.1   Installation of new computers

I was involved in the re-organisation of a learning support centre where one of the tasks was the unpacking and installing of 50 new computers. In a regular weekly phone conversation, the Director of Computing Systems informed me that the new computers had arrived and been installed in the IT room. As I ticked the task off on my project action plan, I thought I would check whether they had been delivered as reported. Walking into the IT room I found the computers were there but had not been installed. The temporary technician had misinformed the director. Fortunately there was still sufficient time to install the computers before students arrived. This example taught me to check that the work has been carried out.

At the implementation stage the critical path analysis becomes very important. The critical path is the series of tasks that are essential if the project is to be completed on time (see Chapter 4). It is vital that the project manager monitors the tasks on the critical path and swiftly introduces remedial action if necessary so the project is delivered on time. The easiest way to do this is to ask people to stop working on non-critical tasks (to the timescale of the project) and move to the critical tasks.

Reporting the project progress

Keep colleagues and stakeholders updated on the progress of the project by thinking carefully about what you want to report to which audience. This is summarised in Table 5.1.

Table 5.1 *The level of detail, frequency and type of communication used for weekly feedback reports on a project's progress, by stakeholder*

Stakeholder	Level of detail	Timing and type of communication
Project manager's manager or director	Regular reports highlighting project progress, and current and potential issues	At regular meetings with line manager or via e-mail
Project team members	As much detail as required to work on the project and understand both the 'big picture' and the detail of their task(s)	Regular, e.g. daily, twice weekly; by e-mail or via project software and/or verbal communications
Project management group	Sufficient information for them to understand project's progress, successes and problems (plus suggested solutions), budget and risk register	Timing is associated with schedule of meetings; bring major problems that arise to attention of the group
Project steering group	Summary information about project progress; highlight main successes, problems (and proposed solutions), budget and risk register	Timing is associated with schedule of meetings; bring major problems to attention of the chairperson to decide how to resolve them
Customers	Report information about milestones completed and any issues that may affect them	As and when required; use e-mail, social media, website etc.
Others, e.g. suppliers	Report information about milestones completed and any issues that may affect them	As and when required; use e-mail etc.

Identifying and managing problems and potential problems

In many respects the project implementation process is about identifying problems or potential problems and developing strategies or interventions for dealing with them. Reiss (1995) provides a useful metaphor for problem solving. He suggests that a project manager is rather like someone standing on the top of a cliff watching a ship come into harbour. The ship is a problem and the harbour is the project manager and team's time and attention. At first the ship is on the horizon and looks small and insignificant. As the ship comes closer it demands attention and may cause the project manager not to see other ships that are now arriving on the horizon. By dealing with the ship that is coming into harbour other problems or ships are gathering on the horizon and will soon move forward into the harbour. The moral is to deal with problems while they are still on the horizon rather than when they arrive in the centre of the project demanding lots of time and attention.

During the implementation stage of a project the manager and team need to be on the lookout for problems or potential problems; these are the most common:

- blockages
- project slippage
- issues
- complex issues.

Blockages
The project manager has to identify and respond to blockages so they don't prevent the project from being completed successfully. Here is a list of some blockages that could arise within a project:

- staff sickness
- delays in recruiting project staff
- staff move to another position
- inaccuracy of estimates of time to carry out work
- unexpected technical difficulties
- failure of contractors to fulfill their commitment
- unexpected delays in building work or installation of systems
- legal problems, e.g. over copyright
- unexpected health and safety issues.

Strategies for dealing with blockages include building in time for problems to the original project plan and/or including a contingency fund. Many project managers build in 20% time for unexpected blockages; if this time is not required, they complete the project early. The next examples show some of the kinds of blockages that may arise during a project.

Case study 5.2   An infestation of fleas

Despite the most well thought-out and detailed project plans, the reality of implementing a project often throws up unexpected events or situations. For example, I was once involved in moving an existing library into a new building. Movement of shelving and stock provided the right environment for the hatching of previously dormant fleas' eggs, and the resulting infestation of fleas caused the library to be closed for a number of days while environmental health officers tackled the problem. Fortunately, we had built two weeks of slack into our contingency plan in the project timetable and although the fleas cost us one of these weeks the delay did not adversely affect the project outcomes.

Case study 5.3   Moving a library

This example by Allen and Bowden (2001) of moving the Dublin City Library illustrates some of the challenges thrown at project managers. It is concerned with delays in transporting stock and accessing lifts:

The major consideration was to keep a steady flow of crates moving between libraries. A system was devised whereby one team would pack the crates and transport them to the new library. When removed from the vans, they would be brought to the relevant floors for shelving. It was envisaged that the empty vans would then return to the old library and the process would recommence. Unfortunately, delays in the schedule commenced almost immediately as it took longer than anticipated to move the containers to the transit vans. It was decided to close one floor to users, and an efficient exit point was re-routed through this area.

Notices were displayed advising users of the closure; however, as this was the quietest time of the year, there was minimum disruption. The solution agreed was to have the movers load the crates and wheel them to the exit point, then slide them down the stairs to the waiting transit vans! A further delay occurred when the movers could not gain easy access to the lifts in the

> new library because of demand by other deliveries of furnishings,
> equipment, fittings etc. This resulted in crates piling up, not only in transit
> vans, but also in both libraries. A solution was eventually found when
> priority was given to the moving company over any other deliveries. This saw
> an end to any further difficulties.   (Allen and Bowden, 2001, 15)

In practice, during the implementation of a project the project manager's time is likely to be spent troubleshooting and problem solving. Project team meetings and management meetings are the place to discuss and, hopefully, resolve blockages.

Project slippage

Slippage occurs when it takes longer than anticipated to complete particular tasks and so becomes impossible to adhere to the project schedule. Once a project manager has realised that the schedule is slipping and different tasks may not be completed on time there are a number of common responses:

- *Obtain additional resources, e.g. obtain more people to work on the project*. While this may appear to be an attractive option, experience in IT projects suggests that simply adding more staff to the project may delay the project even further! The new people have to be trained and given time to work up to speed, which may take time away from the current project team. Carefully introducing a small number of additional people sometimes produces benefits, often when they are given very specific tasks to complete with which they are very familiar.
- *Ask people to work harder or longer hours*. In the short term, this strategy can work. If there is money available in the budget then paying some additional overtime can pay dividends. However, used as a long-term solution this can de-motivate staff and lead to stress, burn-out and an increase in sick leave or staff turnover.
- *Review the project and reduce its scope*. Sometimes slippage can be dealt with by reviewing the scope of the project and either cutting out some of the project outcomes or postponing them until after the project has been officially 'completed'.
- *Accept the slippage and renegotiating a new end date*. Sometimes this is the most sensible course of action as the implementation process

often reveals blockages or problems that had not been anticipated at the planning stage.

Quality issues

The quality of the work should be monitored to ensure that it meets the required standards. The detailed project plan is likely to include information about the quality criteria and how they will be checked. Individuals responsible for monitoring quality need to be proactive, start off their quality processes and procedures from the beginning of the project, and report their findings to the project team and manager frequently. This will enable appropriate adjustments to be made to the working practices of the project team extremely quickly.

Case study 5.4   Assessing quality in a collaborative cataloguing project

Harris and Hinchcliffe (2015) describe a collaborative cataloguing project that involved two academic libraries at Mansfield University and Bloomsburg University in Pennsylvania, USA. They provide a detailed account of their project plan and implantation process, which includes details of their quality assessment criteria (prepared at the planning stage) and a summary of the outcomes presented on a spreadsheet. It has the following headings:

- number of items sent
- number of items checked for project assessment processes
- % of subjects that were valid
- % of subjects that were appropriate
- % of records receiving further work
- call numbers: assignment shelf listing
- correct series call number handling
- correct series tracing practice
- correct series correlation with tracing
- RDA [Resource Description and Access] compliance
- other accuracy points (e.g. typos, transcriptions).

Monitoring the quality of the work during a project is vital and the example given by Harris and Hinchcliffe (2015) demonstrates the level of detail and the attention that needs to be paid to quality in order to ensure the success of the project. The outcome of this type of monitoring can be used to improve the quality of the work throughout the project process. Collecting this type of quantitative data is extremely useful evidence in the reporting, reviewing and evaluation stages of the project.

Complex issues

In complex projects a relatively small change in one part of the system may result in unexpected and unwelcome changes in other parts of it. One of the challenges of managing this type of situation is that changes can be unexpected and sometimes by attempting to put the problem right the project manager and team introduce even greater problems, leading to an unravelling of the entire project plan. In this type of situation it is often best to let the system find a new steady state before attempting to impose order on it. This is illustrated in the following example.

Case study 5.5   The potential unravelling of an information literacy programme

A module called 'Academic and professional practice' was introduced into the undergraduate curriculum of a UK university business school to teach 450 new undergraduates skills in:

- how to study
- information literacy
- how to use ICT
- team work
- quantitative methods.

The module was delivered by a team of eight lecturers, four ICT trainers and two academic librarians. Each week students had to attend a general lecture and an ICT lecture and workshop; in addition to their weekly sessions, every four weeks they attended an information skills workshop and a small group tutorial session. The timetable was complex as students were allocated to their individual sessions on the basis of their degree programme.

In Week 2 severe timetabling clashes took place with the ICT lectures and workshops caused by a change in a timetable within another faculty, which had an impact on the business school students. As a result the whole timetable began to fall apart. The initial response of the module team was to reorganise the ICT lectures and workshops and reallocate all the students to new sessions. This would have taken at least two full days to organise and everyone was already working at full capacity.

However, the team decided to change their approach and instead of allocating students to lectures and workshops explained the situation to the students and asked them to sign up for the sessions that most suited their needs. Over the next four days the students could be seen clustered around notice boards with their timetables. Many of the sign-up sheets became dog-eared as students signed up and then changed their minds about which sessions to attend. Finally, the 450 students had organised themselves into new groups and reported to the teaching team that they much preferred this arrangement as they could now fit their ICT sessions around their other activities. The staff were pleased too – the solution was effective and the students were satisfied. The teaching team decided to provide students with a self-service approach and use this approach to signing up for workshops in future years.

Reviewing the project process

Throughout the project implementation stage there is a need for the project manager and team to review the project process. This enables problems and potential problems to be identified and, ideally, corrected. Many teams include a project review as part of the agenda of their regular meetings. Structures and approaches to reviewing the project are outlined in chapters 2 and 6.

Completing the project

Once the project is approaching completion the project manager and team should focus on managing the following processes and activities:

- project outcomes
- project benefits
- project reports
- loose ends
- hand-over
- celebration.

The project manager and team need to check that all the project outcomes identified at the start of the project have been achieved, and document the benefits achieved. It is likely that there have been unexpected project outcomes and benefits, too, and it is worth itemising and recording them (see chapters 3 and 6). Examples of unexpected project outcomes or benefits include additional publicity for the library and information service, increased confidence in staff, and the development of a 'live' network of like-minded people. Keeping track of the achievement of project benefits and outcomes is important: these may be used to convince potential funders or sponsors in the future that the library and information service is able to deliver the goods.

The project completion stage normally involves writing up the project reports; in large and complex projects, sometimes six months will be set aside for this task at the end of the project. Typically project reports include management reports, finance reports and reports to sponsors. These are all vital as they ensure that all the relevant people (including the information and library profession as a whole) get to hear about and learn from the project. The topic of project reports is covered in some detail in Chapter 6.

It is also important to identify, manage and tie up any loose ends, especially in projects involving contract staff who are likely to leave at the end of the project. Who will deal with late arriving invoices or queries about the project? Who will provide references for the departing project team? How will the stakeholders be informed of the completion of the project? If loose ends are not managed then, the host organisation or staff, who have not been actively involved in the project, will inherit time-consuming and messy work which can cause conflict.

With many information and library projects, e.g. implementing a new information system, moving a library into a new building, there is a hand-over stage when the project ceases to be a project and becomes part of the normal operations. In these types of projects there should be a clear hand-over process so the day-to-day operations manager and team are clearly briefed about managing the new system or building and realise that it is now their responsibility. At the same time the project manager needs to let go of the project and move on to other duties.

One common problem participants on project management courses observe is the difficulty in completing and closing projects. These practitioners said that in their library and information service (predom-inately UK academic and government-based services) they found it difficult to close projects so some projects appeared to creep on over time, devouring resources and de-motivating staff. These are some effective strategies for dealing with this situation:

- identify clear project aims, outcomes, action plan and end date
- raise the issue at staff meetings and ensure staff are instructed to stop work on all project work
- hand over all remaining project work to an individual or small operations team and give them responsibility for tying up loose ends
- formally close the project.

Finally, a good way to end any project is to celebrate the project's successes and the scale of this celebration will vary from tea and cakes through to a large-scale party.

Summary

This chapter focused on project implementation and closure processes. A key message is that even when there is excellent project planning, unexpected events can occur in the implementation process. Consequently, it is best to be alert to them, identify them as quickly as possible and take corrective action.

The next chapter considers the project evaluation process and dissemination.

References

Allen, J. and Bowden, L. (2001) Move Over: moving the DCU library's print material to the new library building, *SCONUL Newsletter*, **24**, 13–16, www.sconul.ac.uk.

Harris, J. and Hinchcliffe, M. (2015) Collaborative Cataloging Pilot Project, *Collaborative Librarianship*, **7** (3), Article 3, http://digitalcommons.du.edu/cgi/.

Reiss, G. (1995) *Project Management Demystified: today's tools and techniques*, 2nd edn, Spon Press.

CHAPTER 6

Evaluation and dissemination

Introduction

This chapter is concerned with project evaluation and methods of disseminating the outcomes of the project. A formal project evaluation process is often required by the funders or sponsors of projects and, in all types of projects, they are an important means of learning from the experience and sharing good practices. Individuals working on small, local projects may feel pressurised to move on to the next project as soon as their current one is complete but if they fail to reflect on and evaluate their work there is the danger that lessons are not learnt and mistakes repeated in later projects.

It is common practice to disseminate the outcomes of a project in order to gain publicity for the project, the library and information service and the parent organisation, and help share good practice and lessons learnt. Dissemination of the outcomes of the evaluation process is considered in the second part of this chapter, which covers reports, websites, social media, community events, presentations at meetings, conference papers, and posters, infographics and e-posters.

Project evaluation

An important part of the project process is project evaluation which is carried out for a number of reasons. As a management tool, it enables the project manager and others to identify their effectiveness, areas of strength and weakness, and lessons for the future. The outcomes of the evaluation process, such as reports or presentations, may be used to disseminate good practice and lessons learnt within the library and information service, their parent organisation, and the wider professional library community. They act as a marketing tool and a means of career progress for individuals. The funders or sponsors of projects normally require some kind of evaluation process to be carried out. Finally a user group or other agency may become involved in evaluating the project.

The project evaluation process entails answering questions such as:

- Did the project achieve its aim and outcomes?
- Did the project achieve any unexpected outcomes?
- What benefits were achieved by the project?
- What was the impact of the project?
- How effective was the project management?
- Was the project delivered on time and within budget?
- Did the project produce work to the required quality?
- What lessons were learnt as a result of the project?
- What will we do differently next time we run a project?

The results of the evaluation will provide evidence of the impact of the project on services, products and people, which may be used in the future to obtain additional funding or support for new projects.

Who will lead the evaluation?

In relatively small and local projects the project manager or a colleague may carry out the evaluation, but the obvious disadvantage of asking project managers to evaluate their own project is that they are likely to be biased (either intentionally or unconsciously) and stakeholders may find it difficult to provide honest feedback if they know that person well. In many large and complex projects the evaluation process is carried out by a member of staff with special responsibility for research or quality issues, or by an external evaluator or a consultant.

If the project is externally funded the funding body or sponsor may require an evaluation by the funder themselves, someone who is contracted by them, or the project team. The funders may be motivated by different reasons, for example to justify their expenditure to their sponsors, to demonstrate the success of the project and its outcomes, and/or to identify areas for improvement (for themselves as funders and the project organisation). The advantages and disadvantages of different people leading the evaluation process are summarised in Table 6.1 on the opposite page.

Table 6.1 *Advantages and disadvantages of different evaluators leading an evaluation process*

Evaluator	Advantages	Disadvantages
Project manager or someone closely involved in the project	Knows the project and its processes Knows the stakeholders Carries out the evaluation as part of their project work	May be biased Participants in the evaluation process may not be completely honest as they know the person May not have very good evaluation skills
Colleague from the same organisation	Understands the context and culture Carries out the evaluation as part of their normal work and doesn't require additional payment Enables them to learn more about the project	May be biased May not have very good evaluation skills
Colleague from the same organisation with a specialist role, e.g. researcher, evaluator, organisational developer	Understands the context and culture Has very good evaluation skills Carries out the evaluation as part of their normal work and doesn't require additional payment Enables them to learn more about the project	May be biased May not have very good evaluation skills
Consultant or external researcher	Ideally has experience of this type of evaluation and project Brings external perspective and experience of evaluating a wide range of projects May have very good evaluation skills	Takes time to identify the appropriate person May be relatively expensive May not understand the specific context or specific culture May not have very good evaluation skills
Person from funding organisation or their representative	Brings external perspective and experience of evaluating a wide range of projects May have very good evaluation skills	May not understand the specific context or culture May not have very good evaluation skills May focus on a very limited set of evaluation criteria May arrive with a set agenda

Approaches to evaluation

Project evaluation processes can be based around different parameters. This section focuses on two approaches: a simple method relevant for small-scale and simple projects involving relatively small numbers of people, and a comprehensive method that may be used within large-scale and complex projects.

Small-scale and/or simple projects

In relatively small-scale and/or simple projects a simple evaluation process is normally sufficient. This may be carried out at stages throughout the life of the project, e.g. as each milestone is reached. One technique that I have used is to ask appropriate people, for example project team members and other stakeholders, four questions:

- What did the project achieve?
- What went well during the project?
- What did you learn from the project?
- What would you do differently if you were to repeat the project?

An easy way of obtaining this information is to divide a piece of flipchart paper, a whiteboard or even a sheet of A4 paper into four and designate a space for each of the questions. Individuals or small groups can then complete the questions and their answers can be included in the final project reports. Alternatively this activity may be carried out using e-mail or through a virtual meeting using Skype or FaceTime. This simple approach is illustrated in Figure 6.1.

What did the project achieve?	What went well during the project?
What did you learn from the project?	What would you do differently if you were to repeat the project?

Figure 6.1 *Simple questions to evaluate a project*

Large-scale and/or complex projects

A more comprehensive project evaluation includes evaluating the project process and the impact of the project from starting point to closure, answering questions such as:

- How effective was the project management structure?
- How effective was the project manager?
- Did the project achieve its aim and objectives?
- Was the project delivered on time and within budget?
- How effective were the project communications?

Process evaluations may be carried out either during the life of the project (and using results to inform the project implementation process) or at the end of the life of the project. In contrast, an impact evaluation process evaluates the impact of the project on different stakeholders, and can be carried out during the project, at its completion, and/or over the medium or long term.

Design of the evaluation process

The design of the evaluation process ideally takes place at the project-planning stage as this helps to ensure that the relevant information is collected during the life of the project. It is worth thinking about the principles behind the evaluation process and answering the following questions:

- Who is responsible for leading and managing the evaluation process?
- What is the purpose of the evaluation process?
- Who has a stake in the project and its evaluation? What are their expectations with respect to the project evaluation?
- What evaluation activities need to take place at each stage in the project?
- How will the different groups of stakeholders be involved in the evaluation process?
- What kinds of evaluation tools will be used in this process?
- Who will carry out the evaluation activities?
- Who will analyse the information obtained during the evaluation process?
- What will the product(s) of the evaluation process be?
- How will these products be disseminated?

Developing the evaluation process involves working through the following steps:

- identify outcomes
- design evaluation methods
- choose methods
- design tools
- collect data
- analyse data
- report and learn from the evaluation process.

The starting point is the project aim and intended outcomes, which should inform the outcomes of the evaluation process. If necessary, go back to the project brief and plan. The next step is to design your evaluation methods so you can measure the outcomes as accurately as possible by identifying the type of data you want to collect, e.g. quantitative or qualitative data, and the detailed information you want to obtain from your work, e.g. library usage statistics, or reading scores before and after the project. Think about who will be involved in this process, e.g. collecting the data and as a participant who provides it, and when this activity should take place. Consider ethical issues including confidentiality and obtain ethical clearance from the relevant body (if required).

Think about how you will measure your desired outcomes. For example, in a survey you may use a series of questions to find out about the impact of your project. If you want to measure usage of a particular aspect of a VLE you may want to measure this via the system analytics. Then design your evaluation tools, e.g. surveys. There is an extensive array of tools that generate data, including:

- project, library and information service, and parent body statistics
- project documentation including minutes of meetings and diaries
- library and information service or parent body documentation, e.g. minutes of meetings and reports
- surveys and questionnaires
- interviews and focus groups
- tests or assessments, e.g. reading scores and examination results
- observation.

The advantages and disadvantages of these different tools are considered in Table 6.2.

Table 6.2 *Advantages and disadvantages of different project evaluation tools*

Tool	Advantages	Disadvantages
Project, library and information service, and parent body statistics	Required statistics may already be collected by library and information service	May require advanced statistical techniques to demonstrate a causal relationship Potential for information overload
Project documentation, including diaries	Very useful for identifying issues and lessons learnt	May not provide the whole picture
Library and information service or parent body documentation	Very useful for obtaining feedback	May not provide sufficient information May be challenging to track down
Surveys and questionnaires	Relatively simple to disseminate	Time-consuming to design May be a low completion rate
Interviews	Provide in-depth information New ideas and thoughts can be followed up	Time-consuming to design and analyse May be challenging to arrange
Focus groups	Provide in-depth information Participants may 'spark off' each other New ideas and thoughts can be followed up	Time-consuming to design Data collection, e.g. video, may be intrusive and put participants off May be challenging to arrange Need an experienced facilitator
Tests or assessments	Very useful if these are already taking place as part of normal activities of institution	Time-consuming to design and administer Stakeholders unlikely to complete them unless mandatory
Observation	Very useful for obtaining information about how people are using a library, the atmosphere, etc.	May be subjective Difficult to analyse accurately

The next step is to collect your data and analyse and draw conclusions from your findings. The type of analysis you will carry out depends on the type of information you have generated:

- Quantitative information is best analysed using simple statistics and measures such as mean, mode, average and range. Information is often best presented using graphs and charts, which enable the reader to quickly identify trends and charts.
- Qualitative information is usually harder to analyse and the simplest approach is often to identify underlying themes and trends, and present them using a simple summary, supported by quotations. The selective use of relevant quotations helps to make reports interesting and they bring out more personal aspects of the experience.

These are some useful sources of information on evaluation and research:

- Bent, M. J. (2016) *Practical Tips for Facilitating Research*, Facet Publishing.
- Boulmetis, J. and Dutwin, P. (2011) *The ABCs of Evaluation: timeless techniques for program and project managers*, John Wiley and Sons.
- Bryman, A. (2012) *Social Research Methods*, 4th edn, OUP.
- Connaway, L. and Powell, R. (2010) *Basic Research Methods in Librarianship*, 5th edn, Libraries Unlimited.
- McNiff, J. (2017) *Action Research*, Sage.
- Stuart, K. and Maynard, L. (2015) *Evaluation Practice for Projects with Young People*, Sage.

Finally, you will report your findings and disseminate them (see later in this chapter).

Measuring the impact of the project

This topic is considered in detail as it is so important for many library and information service project managers who need to measure the impact of the project, for example on library users. Similar approaches are used by library and information services in different sectors as summarised in Table 6.3 opposite. The author had informal discussions with several project managers working in libraries. They said they regularly carry out short-term and medium-term evaluations of the impact of a project but carry out long-

Table 6.3 *Ways of measuring different impacts of a project*
Source: Adapted from Project Outcome
(https://www.projectoutcome.org/about)

	In-project impact	Immediate impact	Medium-term impact	Long-term impact
Objective	To measure impact of project and to inform delivery of project	To measure immediate impact of project	To understand if stakeholders have changed their behaviour because of project	To understand the long-term impact of project on stakeholders (including partners)
When to measure	As soon as project is established	As soon as project is completed	3–6 months after project is completed	9–24 months after project is completed
Evaluation tool	Survey or questionnaire; interviews or focus groups	Survey or questionnaire; interviews or focus groups	Survey or questionnaire; interviews or focus groups	Outcome measurement tool; library and information service statistics
Ideal for	Assessing immediate impact of and gauging reaction to project; generating information to inform the continued progress of project	Assessing immediate impact of and gauging reactions to project; obtaining quotations and basic information, which can be used for publicity	Assessing medium-term impact of project; identifying lessons learnt; informing internal planning; measuring progress towards a strategic goal; providing evidence for funders and other stakeholders (e.g. senior management)	Assessing long-term impact of project; measuring progress towards a strategic goal; providing evidence for funders and other stakeholders (e.g. senior management); providing evidence, which may be used in future bids for funding

term evaluation processes less frequently, as they often lack time or have moved on to managing new or more current issues.

Project managers working in libraries in different sectors use different measures for evaluating the long-term impact of their project. For example, school library projects may be measured using the different tests used in schools for reading and the overall performance of school pupils at different ages. In contrast, a project manager in an academic library may focus on the results of surveys such as the National Student Survey (in the UK) and internal student engagement surveys. In a workplace library, the evaluation process may focus on the success rates of bids for funding by clients, or the number of citations in published reports.

Evaluating a project's success is a complicated business and it is worth project managers of large-scale projects spending time researching current practices within the particular sector. There are many examples of interesting evaluation practices, e.g. Project Impact (https://www. projectoutcome. org), which is focused on the public library sector.

Case study 6.1   Living Voices

The Scottish Poetry Library and the Scottish Storytelling Centre developed the Living Voices project (scottishpoetrylibrary.org.uk) which offers older people a mixture of story, song and poetry to prompt conversation, reminiscence and creative responses. This evaluation process involved an in-project and at-end-of-project methodology consisting of qualitative and quantitative evidence, which was collected using:

- baseline, interim and final surveys with facilitators, volunteers and care homes
- monthly facilitator reflection logs
- volunteer observation sheets
- quartlerly residents' survey and care home observations
- researchers' observations
- interviews with facilitators, volunteers, care home staff and local partners.

An external organisation acted as a 'critical friend' throughout the project and their staff engaged with different aspects of the project, e.g. by attending meetings and observing events, and identified issues which were then fed back via reports and attendance at meetings, to inform the project delivery process. Limitations of the evaluation process were highlighted:

- There was variable content of facilitator logs.
- There was variable content of volunteer observations.
- Residents' surveys did not capture experiences of those with severe dementia.
- It was not possible to track individual responses and impact over time.

- Baseline surveys had to be augmented by additional reflective statements and additional questions were added to the interim and final surveys to provide a more accurate measurement of progress.
- Less than a third of the care homes engaged with the residents' survey and care home observations.

The benefits of the evaluation approach were identified as follows:

- It was responsive and adaptive to the needs of the participants.
- Facilitators benefitted from the practice of keeping a reflective log.
- There was a triangulated approach with findings drawn from many different perspectives.
- The interim reporting stage enabled the project manager to access an extensive range of feedback and evidence, which was then used to inform the project delivery and support.

The evaluation report (Ellison, Christie and Watt, 2014) is 60 pages long and presented in chapters with the following headings:

- Introduction and context
- Impact for Living Voices participants
- Impact for care homes
- Impact for Living Voices facilitators
- Impact for Living Voices volunteers
- Wider impact
- Reflections on the Living Voices model and considerations for the future.

The findings from the project focus on the impact on the different groups identified in the chapter headings and these are brought to life through an extensive range of quotations and images, including tables and figures. There are very few sections containing solid text.

Project dissemination

At the planning stage, it is useful to think about the project dissemination process and incorporate it into the plan and project process. This section considers the following methods of dissemination:

- reports
- websites

- social media
- community events
- presentations at meetings
- conferences papers
- posters, infographics and e-posters.

Reports

Towards the end of many projects, the project manager and team are required to produce a formal report for the steering group, the project funder or another audience. Project reports vary in size from two to three pages through to a whole book. A useful starting point for writing a project report is to start with the project brief.

The structure of reports varies from organisation to organisation, but all reports are likely to include:

- a title
- names of author(s)
- the date written
- acknowledgements
- an executive summary
- an introduction
- a background
- a brief outline of the project
- outcomes
- benefits
- an evaluation of the project
- lessons learnt
- recommendations for action
- a summary
- references
- appendices.

Report writing involves a series of steps:

1   Identify your audience. Who are they and what will they hope to gain from reading your report?
2   Identify an outline structure. If you are working on an externally funded report check whether or not the sponsor has an in-house

style covering report structure and content. This may be available in your contract or on the funder's website.

3   Collect information for the report and start to organise it under headings.

4   Produce a first draft.

5   Ideally take a few days' break from report writing.

6   Return to the report and edit the draft.

7   Ask someone to read the report and obtain their feedback. If you are working in a team you could ask everyone in the team to read it and give you their comments.

8   Edit the report.

9   Re-read the report and edit it for consistency, considering use of language, headings and references.

10   Once you are satisfied with the report think about how to produce it. Different versions (a brochure, a brief summary and a full report) may be required, either paper based or published online. Consider employing the services of a graphic designer to ensure that the report is visually attractive.

11   Once you are satisfied with the finished report disseminate it by:
   – sending copies to sponsors, stakeholders and project team members
   – handing out copies at meetings and conferences
   – sending copies out to other interested parties
   – via the project website.

Case study 6.2   Baltimore Elementary and Middle School Library Project Part 1

The goal of the Baltimore Elementary and Middle School Library Project (known as the Library Project) was 'to transform inner-city school libraries into inspirational spaces in order to impact educational achievement'. It was funded by the Weinberg Foundation, which provided $10 million to build up to 24 libraries (see www.baltimorelibraryproject.org).

The evaluation report covered 2011–2014, during which new libraries were opened in nine schools. It included the following information:

• names of Library Project partners
• an introduction highlighting the schools and key findings
• information about the origins of the project including public school demographics and also the criteria for the initiative

- the research-based principles which shaped the project
- the project model: design and physical space, and resources (including the use of professional library staff)
- names of core funding partners and the funding structure, including building the partnership, relationships and governance structure
- a description of how the Library Project worked: site selection and development; design team; library design; staffing – librarians, clerks, teachers; and resources – technology, collections
- an analysis of progress towards Library Project goals and the challenges of measuring impact, including:
  - changes in reading scores
  - reading fluency data
  - a comparison of pupil attainment across schools (including those not involved in the project)
  - benchmark attainment
  - motivation, climate and readiness for reading
  - feedback from head teachers, teachers and students
  - technological challenges – e-readers, computers, teacher and librarian collaboration
- findings and recommendations, presented with the following headings:
  - best practice in the Library Project model
  - accountability and responsibility
  - an open development and implementation process
  - project direction and oversight
  - strengthening the librarians
  - library resources
  - partnerships
  - parental engagement
  - sustainability
  - evaluation design and implementation
- an appendix containing tables and figures.

This was essentially an interim report of 38 pages as the Library Project is ongoing. It is clearly presented: the text summarises the evaluation of the project, supported by highlights presented in coloured boxes; the under-pinning data is in the appendix. The Library Project's website and use of social media are explored later in this chapter.

Websites

Many projects develop and maintain a website to disseminate information about the project and its activities. If you are involved in a project that decides to market itself using a website, make sure there is adequate staff time in your project plan for this activity, possibly liaising with colleagues in the web team in the library and information service or in the parent organisation.

Information provided on the website may include:

- project aims, benefits and outcomes
- a brief summary of the project
- acknowledgements and information about the project sponsors
- project news
- photographs and video clips
- project reports
- a project blog
- contact details of key project staff.

Case study 6.3   A University of Salford development project

The University of Salford (www.salford.ac.uk) refurbished its main library over an 18 month period and provided the following information about the project on its website.

There was a brief summary of the project, with information presented under five headings:

- How will it affect me?
- Why are we doing it?
- What are we doing?
- Project phases (described using colour coded diagrams)
- Tour (a photographic section).

In addition, library users were informed and supported via chat (a chat session was offered when users accessed the project website), Twitter and a blog. The blog, which appeared to be updated monthly, provided project updates, with an entry written from the student perspective. The library has a Facebook site but this did not appear to be used for communicating information about the development project.

Case study 6.4   Baltimore Elementary and Middle School Library Project Part 2

Earlier in this chapter an outline was given of the structure and content of the interim evaluation report of the Baltimore Elementary and Middle School Library Project (known as the Library Project; www.baltimorelibraryproject. org). The website is multi-coloured in a style that is child-friendly and appropriate for primary schools. More than a third of the page is filled with a sequence of photographs of school libraries. The welcome page includes a request for donations plus access to the interim evaluation report. There are links to Facebook, Twitter and YouTube. The site is structured into six areas:

- prologue (our story begins):
  - inspiration
  - timeline
- plot (why and how?):
  - Baltimore: poverty, children, literacy . . . and the libraries
  - funding already in place
  - how does it work
- characters (partners and sponsors):
  - advisory committee
  - project partners
- setting (selected schools):
  - Year 1 schools
  - Year 2 schools
  - Year 3 schools
  - Year 4 schools
  - Year 5 schools
  - Year 6 schools
- contributors (your role in the story):
  - book drive
- epilogue (our story continues):
  - project evaluation
  - news (in the style of a blog)
  - about us/media
  - contact information.

Social media

Social media is regularly used to raise awareness and disseminate information about projects using tools such as:

- Facebook and LinkedIn

- blogs
- Twitter
- Instagram
- Snapchat
- Steller
- YouTube.

These are described briefly in Chapter 7. If you are considering using social media to promote your project it is worth analysing the current situation and Table 6.4 lists topics and questions to consider. It is normally better to use one form of social media well rather than several haphazardly.

Table 6.4 *Selecting social media*

Theme	Questions
Your institution	1 What is your institutional policy on the use of social media?
	2 Who is responsible for social media within your institution?
	3 Which body or committee will make the key decisions relating to the proposed social media project? How will you obtain their go ahead?
	4 How does your institution use social media? How will your work fit in with this approach?
	5 How does your ICT support the use of social media on computers and networks within the institution?
Yourself and the project	6 Who will be involved in creating and managing the project's use of social media?
	7 What training and development is required to maintain usage of social media?
	8 How much time do you (and your team) have on a daily, weekly or monthly basis to use social media?
	9 Do you have time to develop and maintain a social media presence over the life of the project?
	10 Will you (and your team) be able to find enough interesting content to produce a series of stories, e.g. on a daily, weekly or monthly basis?
	11 What would be the impact of not using social media in your project?
The potential audience	12 Who is your audience? Colleagues, customers, stakeholders or others?
	13 What social media is regularly used by the different groups in your audience?
	14 How will you find out your potential audience's needs?
	15 Will they be interested in your project?
	16 What benefit will they gain from following you on social media?

Table 6.4 *Continued*

Theme	Questions
Content	17 What do you intend to post on social media? Do you have the right type of content to maintain an interesting story on social media? Will you be using text, photographs, infographs, videoclips etc?
	18 What tone will you use on social media? Is this appropriate for your project and organisation? How are your stakeholders likely to respond to this tone?
	19 How will you engage with others on social media? How will you deal with positive feedback? How will you deal with destructive feedback and/or online abuse?
The plan	20 How will you use your knowledge and skills in project management to manage your use of social media?
	21 Is your plan sustainable?
	22 Have you considered how you (and your team) will handle peaks and troughs in your workload?
	23 How will you monitor the responses to your use of social media? Will you use analytics?
	24 How will you evaluate the social media project?
Key factors about different social media – remember social media is constantly changing and developing	
Facebook	Used for creating interest and building reputation. Easy to share stories, images, video clips. Simple to engage with followers.
LinkedIn	Used for creating interest and building reputation. More serious tone than Facebook as its focus is on professional networks rather than social networks. Easy to share stories, images, video clips. Simple to engage with followers.
Blogs	Useful for communicating a more detailed story than is often used on other forms of social media. Comments function enables engagement with followers.
Twitter	Used for breaking news, updates and obtaining quick feedback. Useful if you have a constant flow of short news items or to support a specific event, e.g. conference.
Instagram	Used to share visual images and videos.
Snapchat	Used for sharing chat, messages and images that are short-lived and self-deleting. Useful if you have a constant flow of short news items or to support a specific event, e.g. conference.
Steller	Used for sharing images and creating interest. Calls to action buttons encourage your follower to follow up in some way, e.g. to learn more about your project or to sign up for an event?
YouTube	Useful for sharing project videos.

Community events

One way of disseminating information about your project is to organise a community event and present it to a local audience. Community events can bring together library and information service customers, sponsors, and library and information workers. Special guests, for example celebrities, authors or local dignitaries, may be invited too.

Case study 6.5   Family history day

A branch library in a small town in Yorkshire decided to run a family history day to celebrate the fifth year of its informal family history Friday Morning Club and share its activities and successes with a wider audience. Staff invited the local family history society, a local publisher and two authors to the event. Members of the Friday Morning Club attended, bringing the findings from their research. Library staff had prepared a display of their family history and local history books and on the day demonstrated how to use the family history databases in the library.

The event was a success, attracting more than 30 visitors throughout the day. Five people signed up for the Friday Morning Club and the occasion was reported positively in the local media. Existing members of the Friday Morning Club enjoyed the day and said that it had validated their knowledge and skills in family history research.

Presentations at meetings

Project sponsors and managers may be asked to present their project to a meeting, e.g. a committee or board meeting associated with the parent organisation or the funding body. If you are invited to make a presentation it is worth double checking:

- the time and venue of the meeting
- the purpose of the meeting and your presentation within it
- the audience, their background and expectations
- the time you have been allocated for your presentation
- the availability of ICT, e.g. to present a PowerPoint presentation or an online video or clip
- the value of giving out a handout.

The next section provides advice on the structure of conference presentations, and how to give them and deal with challenging situations, which applies equally to giving a presentation at a meeting. If you are not able to use tools such as PowerPoint it is worth having a handout (if this is acceptable to the chair of the meeting). If not produce a handout for your own use, using the structure outlined in the following section, as this will help you to remember and communicate your main points. You may find it helpful to practise your presentation at one of your regular project meetings in order to obtain constructive feedback before the event.

Conference papers and presentations

Presenting conference papers is an important way to disseminate information throughout the profession. Calls for papers are regularly circulated via the professional networks. If you are interested in presenting your project at a conference the first step is to identify an appropriate conference.

Read the calls for papers and check that your work will fit into any particular conference's theme. If you are uncertain about the suitability of your work contact the organisers and discuss it with them. The next step is normally to send in an abstract or summary of your proposed paper and presentation, which must reach the conference organisers by the closing date. It will be sent to a reviewer or the conference committee, who will decide whether or not to accept your paper.

If your abstract is accepted you may be asked to write and return a completed paper by a set date, normally a month or two before the actual conference. This gives the organisers time to make the papers available to conference participants via a website or USB, and/or to publish the conference papers, e.g. via a website, later. Many conferences don't require a detailed paper but ask for a copy of presentations either before or during the conference, which may be uploaded on to the conference web page.

The organisers will give you a time and location for your presentation and normally ask you for your equipment requirements.

A well prepared presentation delivered with enthusiasm is always well received by an audience. If you give a presentation spend time preparing and thinking about how to deliver it. It is worth checking out earlier programmes of the conference if you have access to them so you gain a feel for the event.

These are some of the benefits of planning and preparing a presentation:

- It gives you confidence so you won't dry up.
- It focuses your thinking on the needs of the audience.
- It helps you to be prepared with appropriate audiovisual aids.
- It helps you to anticipate possible problems and develop contingency plans.
- You are less likely to make basic errors during the presentation.
- Your delivery is more likely to be professional.

Thoroughly research and design your presentation so you are prepared. Consider your audience and answer questions such as:

- Who is the audience?
- How many people will be there?
- What are they likely to want from the presentation?
- What is their knowledge about the subject?

Think about how to structure the presentation. The simplest structure is to divide it into three parts: introduction, main section and conclusion, as shown in the example structure given below.
    This is a typical presentation structure:

1 Introduction
2 Introduce self, acknowledgements, very brief introduction to the topic or theme
3 Background, the library and information service context, reasons and rationale for the project
4 The project, organised around headings such as: funding, staffing, use of ICT
5 Project outcomes
6 Project evaluation
7 Lessons learnt
8 Summary
9 Any questions
10 Close and thank the audience.

This is an alternative presentation structure using the project planning cycle as the framework:

 1 Introduction
 2 Introduce self, acknowledgements, very brief introduction to the
    project
 3 Background, the library and information service context, the project
 4 Getting started
 5 Planning the project
 6 Implementation
 7 Evaluation
 8 Summary
 9 Any questions
10 Close and thank the audience.

Rehearsals are best carried out in front of an audience, perhaps friends and
colleagues at work. If no audience is available consider video- or audio-
taping yourself. Some people (including the author) rehearse in front of
family members and pets!

On the day of the presentation allow yourself plenty of time to find the
venue, meet the conference organisers, and check that all the equipment
is set up and working. If you have not attended the conference before or
the audience is unfamiliar to you spend a little time at other people's
sessions as this will give you a feel for the event and people's expectations.

The best presentations start with a strong and enthusiastic introduction.
Vary the tone and pace of your voice during the presentation to help make
it more interesting. Move around and use hand and arm gestures as a way
of making your presentation lively, but avoid the trap of making repetitive
movements which can be distracting to the audience. Make sure that the
presentation ends on a positive note and does not fade away.

Questions and discussions from the audience are an important part of
any presentation so think about how to handle them. Do you want to take
questions throughout the presentation or leave them until the end?
Inexperienced presenters usually find it easier to leave questions until the
end so they can stick to their plan and not be distracted or diverted
throughout the presentation. Whatever you decide, let the audience know
how you will handle questions at the start of the presentation. I always
start by taking questions from people who look helpful and supportive as
this helps to set a positive tone to the session. It is easy to control the
number of questions you will answer by using phrases such as 'There is
time for one more question'.

Sometimes challenging situations arise during presentations. Table 6.5 provides some simple guidelines for handling common challenging situations.

Table 6.5 *Ways of managing challenging situations*

Situation	Possible responses
Someone asks a question that you are unable to answer	Be honest and say that you cannot answer the question; ask questioner to contact you after the session as you will try to find out the answer
One person starts to ask lots of questions and appears to want to take over the session	Explain that time is short and you want to give a wide range of people the opportunity to ask questions; offer to meet later
Two members of the audience start an argument with each other	Don't take sides; if appropriate, suggest that they agree to disagree and move on to another topic
Someone challenges the fundamental basis of your project, e.g. if it was externally funded they may suggest that the money would have been better spent on a different project	Don't get into an argument; state that you were sponsored to complete the project and that is the focus of your presentation; suggest that they contact the funders if they wish to discuss the criteria by which projects were selected for funding
Someone suggests that you would have managed the project better if you had used a different project methodology, e.g. PRINCE2® or Agile	Explain that there are many different project methodologies and you selected the one that appeared to be most appropriate for your specific context and project; you have now learnt the advantages and disadvantages of the methodology and would take their comments into consideration the next time you are involved in project work

At the end of the presentation remember to thank the audience for their time and participation. Afterwards, ask for feedback from colleagues in the audience and read their evaluation forms. Use this information to help you to improve your presentations in future. Make contact with those people whom you promised to contact. This is very crucial as being part of a professional network is a valuable part of professional life and helps support career development.

Posters, infographics and e-posters

Many conferences include poster sessions, which enable delegates to present their work in a colourful and imaginative way using visual images. Typically, printed posters are likely to be A1 size (the same size as flipchart paper). During a poster session, the author of the poster stands in front of it and discusses its contents with other conference participants. Although relatively time-consuming to produce, the poster may be re-used after any individual event.

Infographics (or information graphics) provide opportunities to present complex information using graphics with the aid of a specialist tool (see for example http://infogr.am). They are particularly useful in presenting summary information, e.g. about the number of items in a library, miles of shelving, or numbers of e-journals available.

There are good examples of different types of infographics posters used in libraries at http://ebookfriendly.com/libraries-matter-library-infographics and https://librariandesignshare.org/category/infographics. It is possible to obtain free templates and support for developing infographics. Carry out a quick search on a search engine to find an extensive range of resources on designing and producing infographics. There is also a growing number of books on the subject, e.g. Crane (2015) and Creighton (2015).

E-posters enable library and information workers to develop rich presentations with links and digital media via a SMART board or large screen (see for example www.eposters.net). Molloy and Boyle (2014) write about the benefits of using e-posters, and their potential for re-use within the library and information service. However, they comment that it can be very time-consuming to produce an e-poster and it is best to limit them to a relatively small number of slides, e.g. ten PowerPoint slides.

Summary

This chapter has explored the evaluation process for small-scale, simple projects and large-scale, complex projects. The outcomes of the evaluation process are an important means of learning from the experience, formally reporting the project's outcomes and impact within your organisation and to external bodies such as funding organisations, and sharing your experiences with the wider library and information profession. The second part of this chapter considered ways of disseminating the outcomes of the evaluation process, through: reports, websites, social media, community events, presentations at meetings, conference papers, posters, infographics and e-posters.

The next chapter considers the use of ICT to support project management.

References
Crane, B. (2015) *Infographics: a practical guide for librarians*, Rowman and Littlefield.

Creighton, P. M. (2015) *School Library Infographics: how to create them, why to use them*, Tech Tools for Learning, Libraries Unlimited.

Ellison, S., Christie, I. and Watt, G. (2014) *Evaluation of the Living Voices Pilot*, Blake Stevenson, www.scottishpoetrylibrary.org.

Molloy, J. and Boyle, S. (2014) Eposter Design: a leap into the unknown, *SCONUL Focus*, **62**, 24–7, www.sconul.ac.uk.

CHAPTER 7

Using ICT to support project work

Introduction

This chapter explores the use of ICT to support project management. ICT is used to help plan, organise and manage the project process, and to communicate within the project team and to the wider group of stakeholders.

There are a number of approaches to using ICT to support and help manage project work:

- *Everyday ICT tools* such as e-mail and spreadsheets work well for relatively simple projects and those that involve a small number of people.
- *Specialist project management software*, either purchased or free open source, is vital for large-scale or complex projects, particularly if they involve a large number of project workers. This software can also be useful for small-scale projects, and some people who use it first on small-scale projects find it a good preparation for using it later on larger-scale or more complex projects.
- *Collaborative tools* enable individuals and teams to communicate with each other, share documents and provide online editing facilities. These may be used in all sorts of projects.
- *Social media, crowdfunding, crowdsourcing and a range of commonly used tools* can be used in all sorts of projects. Crowdfunding is considered in Chapter 8, and crowdsourcing is explored in Chapter 9.

Everyday ICT tools

The easiest way to manage a simple project is to use the ICT tools that are an everyday part of your working life. A typical example is shown in Table 7.1 overleaf, which is followed by a case study.

Table 7.1 *Everyday ICT tools for managing simple projects*

Tasks	Use of ICT
General documentation, e.g. project brief	Word processing
Planning the schedule	Spreadsheet
Monitoring the schedule	Spreadsheet
Monitoring milestones	Electronic diary
Budget	Spreadsheet
Communicating with colleagues	E-mail
Communicating with customers or stakeholders	E-mail, website, blog, Twitter

Case study 7.1   Managing a library move

Sarah works in a voluntary organisation in Birmingham where she is the sole information officer. The library (5000 books and journals, five computers, a photocopier and ten desks with chairs) is moving to a new building and the overall move is being led and managed by the charity's operations manager. Sarah decided to manage her part of the project using basic ICT tools as she does not have time to learn how to use a new software package and thinks the move is relatively straightforward. Sarah starts the process by brainstorming what needs to happen in the move (Figure 7.1).

Inform customers	Pack books	Check size of new office	Inform customers about closure on day of move
	Order crates	Check to find out if there is a budget for the move – buy new furniture?	Arrange party to welcome customers to new library
Contact IT department about phone and IT cabling requirements	Check with main office move manager about dates for library move	Work out new office plan	Produce posters to inform people of new location
Contact colleagues in other workplace libraries to see if they have any tips for the move	Check location of kitchen, toilets etc in new location	Weed books	Work out comms relating to move

Figure 7.1 *Results of a brainstorming session*

Sarah then transferred these ideas onto an Excel spreadsheet (Figure 7.2). She printed this out and kept it beside her desk, crossing off each task as it was completed. After the move, Sarah attended the final task group meeting, which reviewed the project and lessons learnt. Her feedback included the following observations:

- The task group meetings and e-mail discussions between meetings were very useful as she felt that she was kept informed and had a say in the move.
- She found her spreadsheet chart useful but it did not include all the chasing up that she had to do, e.g. crates had not arrived on time, so she had to chase up the IT department a number of times. She found that she spent much more time chasing up issues than she had expected.
- She was disappointed that she wasn't given a budget for new furniture as she thought the new space was wonderful but the old furniture looked a bit shabby. However, she understood that times were hard.
- Her welcome party had worked well and was attended by 24 people over the three-hour period. She used the party and the move to generate additional publicity for the library.
- Overall, she was pleased with the move – the library was now in a much better location and her customers seemed pleased with it. She had received no complaints.

TASKS	6 Feb	13 Feb	20 Feb	27 Feb	6 Mar	13 Mar	20 Mar	27 Mar
Check with ops manager	■							
Attend task group			■		■			■
Check possible budget	■							
Check size of new office	■							
Contact ILS colleagues	■							
Order crates meetings		■						
Contact IT department		■						
Visit new space		■						
Inform customers		■						
Work out new plan			■					
Weed books			■			■		
Pack books				■	■			
Arrange welcome party				■				
Inform customers of closure					■			
Produce re-direction posters					■			
Check all arrangements						■		
MOVE!							■	
Welcome party meetings								■

Figure 7.2 *Spreadsheet showing plan for a library move*

Project management software

Project management software, sometimes called task management or project portfolio management, enables you to carry out the following types of activities:

- plan the project, establish the schedule, identify the critical path, allocate resources
- view the project and obtain a range of reports
- track progress and identify issues
- manage cost reporting and budgeting
- support team communications e.g. via e-mail, text messages or an app
- manage multiple projects.

Project management software is available for use on a wide range of ICTs, and through desktops, laptops, the Cloud and apps. The development of project management apps means that information and communications relating to the project is readily accessible to the project team. The advantages and disadvantages of using project management software are outlined in Table 7.2.

Table 7.2 *Advantages and disadvantages of using project management software*

Advantages	Disadvantages
Most packages are relatively easy to use	Time taken to learn software
Provides a relatively simple way of managing project information	Data input can be time-consuming
Provides many ways of viewing the project, producing reports and identifying issues	May experience information overload
Essential for managing large projects	May be too complex and time-consuming for small projects
Provides a single source of information for the project, which may be accessed by different people	People are treated as 'resources' rather than valued colleagues in the language of some software packages
Provides a professional image	Provide a means of managing the information and it is only useful if the data is accurate and up-to-date.

Project managers and team workers use hundreds of types of software packages. MS Project is widely used. It provides an extensive range of functions but is rather expensive. There are many examples of open source packages, but although they provide free access to a few basic project management tools, e.g. task management, a subscription may be required to access more sophisticated features.

Many organisations have a preferred project management package, which is useful as you do not need to select a package and there should be in-house experience and help available to you. In other organisations staff select and purchase the software, which can be very challenging because of the choice available. Some factors to take into account when selecting project management software are outlined in Table 7.3.

Table 7.3 *Factors to consider when selecting project management software*

Features	Characteristics
Desktop or web-based	• Desktop – often transfers large files faster and has single fixed-cost licence • Web-based – easy access for project managers and team members who are either mobile or at a different location; specialist apps provide a convenient means of keeping up to date
Open source or purchased software	• Open source – many are excellent but check them out carefully. Often limited set of functions, back-up and support • Purchased software – many have excellent support and training opportunities
Usability	• Is it easy to use? • Is the structure and layout clear and intuitive? • What type of help is available within the package? • Is it available via an app? • Does it enable project information and images to be exported to other packages, e.g. Word or PowerPoint?
Level of complexity	• Does it provide the features needed for your project? • How many of the features don't you need? Some project management packages are very complex and you may only need 5–10% of their functionality
Specific functions	• Does it enable you to develop Gantt (or equivalent) charts? • Does it enable you to develop PERT (or equivalent) charts? • Does it automatically identify the critical path? • Does it enable you to identify and display who has been allocated each task? • Does it enable you to balance the scheduling of staff's workload – resource levelling? • Does it enable you to produce a list of tasks completed and tasks outstanding? • Does it provide reports on milestones achieved? • Does it support team communications, e.g. via e-mail or text messages, reminding individuals to complete tasks and/or update the information on the project plan?

Some software is designed to match particular approaches to project management, as shown in Table 7.4. Be aware that many of the products provide support for all three of the main approaches to project management, even though their publicity material is focused on one approach.

Table 7.4 *Software packages for different approaches to project management*

Project management	Purchased	Open source
General	Basecamp Huddle MS Project Podio SmartDraw®	Asana Freedcamp LibrePlan MyCollab Odoo OpenProject ProjectLibre Redmine Zoho projects
PRINCE2®	CorePM Easy Projects PRINCE2®	Project in a Box
Agile	Atlassian JIRA Easy Projects LiquidPlanner Trello SmartDraw®	Agilefant Orangescrum OpenProject Project in a Box Taiga

Before selecting project management software it is well worth reading reviews in the computing and project management professional literature and on websites, and exploring the library and information literature, to find out about commonly used packages and their advantages and disadvantages. As with all ICT, it is a rapidly changing field.

Planning a project using project management software

Project management software is used to plan projects by inputting the following information: project tasks, duration, links with other tasks, milestones and resources (about the team workers who are allocated tasks and the project finances). The amount of information required at this stage depends on the sophistication and capabilities of the software. This is the most basic information required:

- name of task
- who it is assigned to

- the start and end date (or the number of working days it will take to complete)
- the dependency of one task to another.

This information is then used to produce a variety of project-planning documents. For example, using SmartDraw® (www.smartdraw.com) to plan the simple and small-scale e-learning project presented in Chapter 4 resulted in the following outputs:

- a Gantt chart (Figure 7.3)
- a task list for the whole team (see Figure 7.4)*
- a project timeline (see Figure 7.5)* (*on the next page).

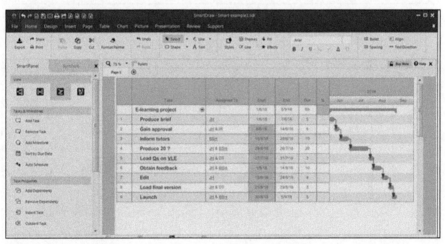

Figure 7.3 *Example of using SmartDraw® to list tasks for an e-learning project*
Source: SmartDraw® (www.smartdraw.com)

In most project management packages, once the basic information is produced it may be used to produce a number of outputs. These vary from software to software and are likely to include at least a calendar (or timeline) and a Gantt chart. The more sophisticated packages that are required for large-scale or complex projects provide the following:

- a calendar showing working days, holidays and weekends
- a Gantt chart
- a PERT diagram, including the critical path

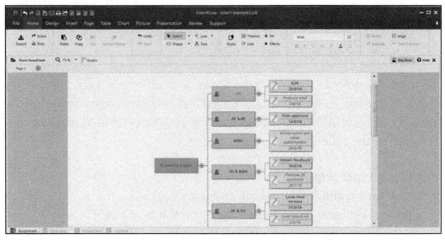

Figure 7.4 *Example list of assignments created using SmartDraw®*
Source: SmartDraw® (www.smartdraw.com)

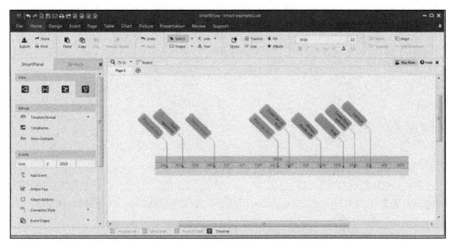

Figure 7.5 *Example of a project timeline produced using SmartDraw®*
Source: SmartDraw® (www.smartdraw.com)

- task allocation – who is doing what, when
- resource levelling – identify who is over- or under-scheduled and then manually or automatically level or smooth out the allocation of people to tasks over time.

Once you have input this basic information update it as the project is implemented. As long as the project information is kept up to date the following reports and support will be available:

- reports on tasks completed and tasks outstanding
- reports on milestones achieved
- support for team communications, e.g. via e-mail or text messages, reminding individuals to complete tasks and/or update the information on the project plan
- support for project meetings, e.g. reports on different aspects of the project.

This information is often available in a variety of formats, e.g. as pdf files, lists, bar charts and other visual images, and it is normally possible to export this information to other tools, e.g. Word, Excel or PowerPoint. Therefore the project management software is extremely useful when managing a project implementation process and communicating it to the different groups of stakeholders.

Collaborative tools

Many sophisticated project management packages provide a range of collaborative tools, and these are often linked to the project plan. Some project managers use collaborative tools if they are working on a project that involves extensive collaboration, e.g. in developing shared resources or learning materials with many teams or institutions, either in one country or across continents. There are many collaborative tools available and typically these enable you to:

- organise meetings
- communicate with each other, either singly or in groups
- share and discuss information and ideas
- work together, e.g. on a report or other document
- co-ordinate activities.

Online tools enable you to carry out an extensive range of activities. Table 7.5 provides a summary of current collaborative tools for different functions. The choice of tools depends on your working context and the size and complexity of your project. For simple projects involving a small team Skype and Google Docs may be sufficient. In larger and more complex projects it is worth considering using software that integrates a whole range of collaboration and project management tools. Again, this is a rapidly changing field so carry out up-to-date research to identify the most appropriate tools for your working context and project.

Table 7.5 *Collaborative tools for different functions*

Function	Collaborative tools
Organise meetings	Doodle Congregar Stickymoose
Edit documents	Google Docs Zoho productivity apps Etherpad TitanPad iWork
Share files	Dropbox Google Docs Box TeamDrive Dropmark
Share and organise links	Diigo Pinterest Pearltrees
Online meetings	Skype FaceTime Vyew MashMeTV Google Hangouts GoToMeeting MeetingBurner Slack Talky

Social media

Many libraries use social media and there is a growing research base on ways it can be exploited. Hofschire and Wanucha (2014) discuss a survey of social media adoption in public libraries: 'Results suggest that social media . . . will continue to grow, although the ways in which these technologies will be implemented are uncertain.' In particular, they suggest that social media is predominately used for marketing and promotion. Wise (2016) provides a practical guide to the use of social media. Although it is written from a business perspective much of what she writes is very relevant to project work in libraries and information services.

Some project managers and team members use social media to communicate with their colleagues and/or their wider community of stakeholders. It is a very challenging area to research and write about as it is constantly changing and developing. A useful source of information and ideas in the context of library and information work is Phil Bradley's website (www.philb.com). If you are working collaboratively on international projects (see Chapter 9) be aware that some social media tools are not available in some countries.

Two uses of social media are explored later in this book: crowdfunding is considered in Chapter 8 and crowdsourcing is explored in Chapter 9.

These are some commonly used examples of social media used in project work in libraries:

- Facebook and LinkedIn – as an open group to promote the project or as a closed group for project workers to communicate with each other; Facebook Canvas – to help businesses share stories and images
- Blogs – to communicate project news to a wider audience, e.g. co-workers, customers and other stakeholders
- Twitter – to announce project news and engage stakeholders, e.g. during a consultation period or as part of a conference or other event; Twitter Moments – to produce a series of tweets to create a slideshow story, which may include photos, videos and other images
- Instagram – to share project news; Instagram Stories can include photos, videos etc.
- Snapchat – to share messages and images
- Steller – to combine images, videos and texts to create formatted stories
- YouTube – to share a project video.

These are some example uses of social media in project work:

- *Facebook* is often used to raise awareness and funding, e.g. for the Street Library Ghana Project, or for publicity, e.g. Little Free Library Project in the UK. A quick survey of Facebook suggests that it is often used to publicise library projects, particularly in the voluntary sector, but these sites are then abandoned at the end of the project often without any closure information. Closed groups may be used for people working on a specific project.
- *LinkedIn* may be used to raise awareness about a project, often when an individual posts an article about a project they are working on. Open or closed groups can be used as a communications tool. In

practice, it appears that closed groups are more commonly used for library project work than open groups.

- *Blogs* are commonly used to disseminate project information at regular intervals, e.g. weekly. A typical example is a blog at the University of Salford used to inform students, staff and other stakeholders about the library redevelopment project at the Clifford Whitworth Library. It provides clear information about forthcoming and imminent changes, and includes a student's perspective of the work. Readers may comment on the individual blog entries or are signed to other contact points (see http://blogs.salford.ac.uk/library-development-project).

- *Twitter, Instagram, Snapchat or Steller* are used to disseminate news and information about projects and their progress. For example, the Library of Birmingham tweeted on 23 January 2017, 'The Library of Birmingham and the British Library received £91,700 of National Lottery funding to present Documenting Histories, a partnership project celebrating the important role South Asian culture has played in forming Birmingham's history and identity' (see https://twitter.com/libraryofbham?lang=en). More detailed information about the new project was available in a blog on the library website at http://libraryofbirmingham.com.

- *YouTube* is used to post videos on current and completed library projects, especially large-scale or architectural projects e.g. Delft University of Technology Library (https://www.youtube.com/watch?v=qAtHkVZk8W8).

In Chapter 6, Table 6.4 provides a checklist with a set of questions to help you decide whether or not to use social media to support your project.

Case study 7.2   Using social media to build a community

Rossman and Young (2015), based in the Montana State University Library, describe research into a social media project that involved the following goal and strategies:

> Fundamentally, we aimed to build a sense of community for our users, and we would employ strategies of personality and interactivity. People would follow us because we would bring an authentic sense of personality to our regular social media posts and interactions. From there, we would build a valuable and rewarding sense of connection and community together with our users.

The Montana State University Library has an internal committee, the Social Media Group (www.lib.montana.edu/about/social-media), which works with stakeholders and the wider online community using social media activities, and identifies new approaches to increasing the library's social media profile. The website states that it strives to:

1 Engage a growing and active university community by expressing through certain high-trafficked social media channels the services, collections, and personality of the library and the library employees.
2 Expand beyond the concept of 'Library as Building' by creating interactive online information-sharing spaces that emphasize 'Library as Services and 'Library as Resources' to students, researchers, faculty, and to the greater library, university, and Montana community.
3 Cultivate these spaces to be consistent with the concept of the library learning commons, recognizing that library-users are crafting online lives that reflect and interact seamlessly with their off-line world.
4 Develop relationships through social media that will ultimately allow our community to discover a library that is more relevant, approachable, valuable, and vital, with resulting increases in foot traffic, virtual and in-person reference interactions, and overall awareness and use of library services and library resources.
5 Serve as social media leaders on campus and in the community by developing expertise through research, real-time interactions, platform and trend awareness, instructional and teaching sessions, engaging discussion across campus social media constituencies, and successful online community building.
6 Conduct research regularly to assess the impact and value of the MSU [Montana State University] Library's social media activity across all platforms.

The Social Media Group developed a social media guide, which identifies the number of ways in which the library uses Facebook, Twitter – Library, Twitter – Scholarship, Pinterest and Instagram. For example, its guide to Instagram covers the following themes:

• community focus – campus and local Bozeman area community, alumni
• goal – raise awareness of library resources (special and digital collections, spaces); build community around campus history
• values – history (Bozeman, campus, library)
• activity focus – historical content

- tone and tenor – light-hearted
- posting frequency – once or twice weekly
- posting categories – reference question series (#letmelibrarianthatforyou), historical photos with context, furniture and building highlights, student highlights, nature and landscapes
- posting personnel – named individual.

Rossman and Young (2015, 22) conclude their article with a set of guidelines to help librarians and information workers to explore and establish their own social media community:

- Create and document a plan for engaging on social media.
- Listen to your community.
- Adapt your plan as you learn.
- Provide personality-rich content that invites two-way interaction.
- Make your content easily shareable with social media optimization.
- Create a social media mascot that represents your library's unique character.
- Use analytics applications such as Twitter's analytics to provide insights.

Case study 7.3   Calculating value: a digital library's social media campaign

Lamont and Nielsen (2015) provide a research article which describes how librarians at San Diego State University embarked on a social media campaign focused on promoting the library's digital archival and historical collections. They also wanted to assess the value of the campaign and whether or not the benefits were greater than the costs. The campaign used Tumblr and Pinterest, and their usage was evaluated using Google Analytics and database reports. Overall, the campaign did not have a big impact on usage of digital collections and did not present good value.

The authors concluded that the initial campaign provided a useful learning experience but they needed a longer testing period. In future, they would promote relevant content and respond promptly to users. They had plans to hire a student to blog and tweet to help enhance the tone and content of the messages. In addition, librarians are promoting the digital librarian's campaign through the library's blog and Twitter account to encourage more interactivity with others. The authors conclude:

As this experiment pointed out, the initial investment may not result in a high return, but librarians should be prepared to be flexible, to try new media platforms, to approach different audiences and to be available to the users. While promoting digital collections on social media has not proven its value at this point, further experimentation may prove differently.

(Lamont and Nielsen, 2015, 111)

Case study 7.4   Social technologies in public libraries in Australia

Smeaton and Davis (2014) carried out a study of social media in two Australian public libraries and explored staff attitudes and organisational culture. Using interviews and documentary analysis, they identified five recurring themes in the two case studies.

When creating communities – facilitate communities of interest through social technologies – it is important:

- to facilitate the growth of communities
- to invite participation and engagement
- to be at the centre of the community
- to be approachable and inclusive
- to have strong customer service ethics.

When using social technologies as way to connect with users in their own space it is important:

- to be outside the library building
- to extend the library from physical to virtual spaces
- to be personable and present the human side of the library
- to avoid corporate speak
- to give the library a personality.

When using social technologies to allow users to have greater say in library direction and generate content the library staff worked:

- to invite participation and engagement
- to post what is interesting to the user (rather than the library staff)
- to target messages
- to design posts to provoke engagement
- to use different platforms in different ways to allow maximum engagement

- to share control and allow users to become co-creators.

In order to foster an organisational culture that uses social technologies to create a participatory service, the organisations:

- valued their employees
- provided a supportive working environment
- encouraged innovation
- encouraged thinking about the future
- understood the importance of learning
- understood that 'social media is not an exact science' and that there was a constant need to review and develop practice.

The study had mixed findings on staff's skills in using social media when implementing social technologies:

- Some staff were highly skilled in using social media in both their professional and private lives.
- Other staff were reluctant to use social media and had limited or no exposure to it.
- It was important to provide 'play time' to enable staff to develop their confidence and skills in using social technologies.
- Play and exploration was used in social media training sessions.
- There was a need to get staff to recognise the use of social media as a normal part of their job rather than an add-on.
- There was value in making the use of social media routine for staff.
- There was a need to accept a change in the relationship with users as they become co-creators.

Case study 7.5   Personal reflection on the use of ICT to support a project by a librarian working in the voluntary sector

A colleague working in the voluntary sector provided me with this case study about her use of ICT to support a relatively small-scale project:

I work as a librarian for a national charity which is in the field of health and social care. I have been in my role for 5 years and love it. We recently merged with another charity and I had the job of merging the two libraries. Unfortunately, the librarian from the other organisation was made redundant which upset us all but we just had to get on with the job. I wanted to use project management tools and techniques, and bought myself a book on the subject. It was helpful and I think I learnt the basics from it. We haven't a budget for attending external courses. I wanted to use project management software – as a way of developing my skills and improving my CV – and investigated it via Google. I found that the free software was too basic for my needs and we had no budget to buy one of the better ones. I realised that I was spending too much time on this research. I decided to use Excel and produced a table of tasks (a Gantt chart) and I worked out the critical path using sticky notes. This I marked on the spreadsheet by making the critical tasks appear in red and bold. I then printed off a copy for my two assistants and myself. We then used this printout to keep on top of the work. It was a relief each time we were able to cross off a task. In terms of communications, I kept it simple – an e-mail on a fortnightly basis to colleagues telling them about the progress of the project. I only used Facebook (the charity uses it a lot) and this was partially successful – I got some nasty feedback from people who supported the charity that merged with us and they were clearly still upset by the change. I responded as best I could given the circumstances. Overall, the project went well and I realised that I had used some of the ideas I learnt from the project management book.

Summary

This chapter explored the use of ICT to support project work. It considers the use of everyday tools, such as e-mail and spreadsheets, to help manage simple or small-scale projects; specialist project management software, which is vital for large-scale and complex projects; and collaborative tools, which enable individuals and teams to communicate with each other and share documents, and provide online editing facilities; and social media. Two aspects of social media are considered later in this book: crowdfunding in Chapter 8 and crowdsourcing in Chapter 9.

ICT is a rapidly changing field and readers are advised to spend some time researching and testing potential tools before they commit to using them as part of a project.

References

Hofschire, L. and Wanucha, M. (2014) Public Library Websites and Social Media: what's #trending now?, *Computers in Libraries*, 4–9, http://tefkos.comminfo.rutgers.edu/.

Lamont, L. and Nielsen, J. (2015) Calculating Value: a digital library's social media campaign, *The Bottom Line: Managing Library Finances*, **28** (4), 106–11.

Rossman, S. W. H. and Young, D. (2015) Using Social Media to Build Community, *Computers in Libraries*, May, 18–22, www.infotoday.com/cilmag/.

Smeaton, K. and Davis, K. (2014) Social Technologies in Public Libraries: exploring best practice, *Library Management*, **35** (3), 224–38.

Wise, L. (2016) *Relax! It's Only Social Media: a no-nonsense guide to social networking for you and your business*, Amazon Media.

CHAPTER 8

The money side of projects

Introduction

The ability to understand and manage the money side of projects is an essential skill for all project managers. Although some library and information service projects are carried out within normal departmental budgets, many are funded by external sources so information workers become involved in obtaining external funding and then managing a budget. The focus of this chapter is funding and obtaining funds from external sources, including crowdfunding. The chapter also covers current approaches to funding, technical terms, external sources of funding, bidding and tendering for projects, managing the finances, and audits.

Current approaches to funding

Organisations in the public and private sector are facing financial challenges, so there is a shortage of funding, particularly for the library and information service. Traditionally, many library and information services have had access to external funds through competitive bidding.

Funding is available from a wide range of sources, including international organisations, central and regional governments, businesses, charitable and other special funds. However, these sources are decreasing and there is greater competition for funding. Consequently, funders are looking for excellent and extremely convincing applications. In recent years, new ways of generating funding have developed as a result of social media, and an important new potential source for library and information services is crowdfunding (see the section 'Crowdfunding' later in this chapter).

External funding organisations

Keeping up to date with possible sources of funding is a challenging task. This section alerts readers to the wide range of funding sources currently available in the UK but does not attempt to provide a comprehensive list of all potential sources. Readers in other countries are likely to obtain guidance from their professional body or other agencies. For example, the American Library Association provides a Frontline Fundraising Toolkit (see www.ala.org).

There is a diverse range of sources of funding and the types and availability of funds is constantly changing. Table 8.1 shows examples of funding bodies. Funding opportunities change over time as the priorities and access to funds of funding organisations change. Therefore anyone who is considering bidding for funding must do extensive research to identify current sources of funding and their current detailed requirements. Many information workers use specialists who provide up-to-date information and advice on funding matters. For example, local authorities typically employ specialist staff with expertise in funding and funding applications in their economic development units, while universities often have a centralised research and development department that provides access to this type of specialist information. Individual consultants working in this field offer their services and expertise in funding applications too.

Table 8.1 *Examples of funding organisations*

Organisation	Website
Arts Council	www.artscouncil.org.uk
Big Lottery Fund	https://www.biglotteryfund.org.uk/funding/Awards-For-All
Carnegie UK Trust	www.carnegieuktrust.org.uk
Directory of Social Change	www.dsc.org.uk
Heritage Lottery Fund	www.hlf.org.uk
National Literacy Trust	www.literacytrust.org.uk
School Funding Service	http://schoolfundingservice.co.uk/grants-for-school-library
TownsWeb Archiving	https://www.townswebarchiving.com/2015/12/ sources-funding-for-heritage-digitisation-projects
Wellcome Trust	https://wellcome.ac.uk/funding

Funding is available from an extensive range of sources for information and library workers based in the UK, though it may take a lot of time to identify an appropriate source of funding for a project. These are some useful organisations and resources to investigate:

- the Heritage Alliance
  (www.theheritagealliance.org.uk/fundingdirectory)
- Trustfunding (www.trustfunding.org.uk)
- the Directory of Social Change (www.dsc.org.uk), or Lilly, D. and
  Zagnojute, G. (2015) *The Directory of Grant Making Trusts*,
  Directory of Social Change
- the Institute of Fundraising (www.institute-of-fundraising.org.uk/
  home).

Working in partnership

Project managers are increasingly asked to lead project teams that involve library and information workers as well as professional colleagues from within the same or different sectors. Finance is often a key driver for partnership working as it offers opportunities that attract funding in a way that is not available for an individual library or information service. The finances often drive the project as monies may be available and must be used up within a specified time period. In addition, partnership working offers opportunities to share resources, e.g. through shared services as discussed in Chapter 10.

The appearance of 'calls to tender' sometimes results in frenzied activities as individuals in organisations attempt to find appropriate partners and establish a partnership that will enable them to bid successfully for funds. Partners may be sought within the same or different sectors, and many projects require cross-sector and multi-professional working. Establishing new partnerships in haste can lead to potential difficulties later on in the relationship. Individuals and organisations with a track record in gaining external funds successfully normally have well established networks with potential partners. The relationships essential for successful funding applications and project working are already firmly established and can be demonstrated in the funding application. It is therefore worth starting to build up appropriate networks and contacts well before the appearance of any calls to tender. Working in partnership is considered in more detail in Chapter 10.

Technical terms

This section provides information on some of the terminology used in financing projects, the terms are arranged in alphabetical order. Please note that these are not legal definitions of the terms but explanations to help you understand them. Consequently, it is very important that you check with your procurement and finance departments so you understand exactly what is required from your organisation's procurement and financial policies and practices.

Audit

An audit is an official examination of the project's records, particularly financial records, to verify that they are correct and meet the requirements of the project funder or parent organisation. An audit is normally carried out by a professional accountant.

Budget

The budget is a description of a project that explains how the project manager will use the finances to achieve the action plan. The project budget is initially produced as an estimate of the expected income and expenses of the project. It is itemised under headings such as: staffing, ICT, travel. Avoid using headings such as 'miscellaneous' or 'other items'. It is important to be realistic in working out a budget and obtaining evidence-based figures to help ensure that it is accurate. Once the budget is approved it sets the total amount of money required for the project.

Business plan

A business plan establishes the aims and objectives of the organisation and their link to the proposed project. It may include information about the organisation itself, including its legal status, strategic plan, policies and practices. It includes the aims and outcomes of the project, the need for the project and its financial support, a series of targets (e.g. type and number of users and volume of traffic on a website). The core of the business plan is the budget and cash flow (see elsewhere in this section).

Cash flow

Cash flow means the amount of money coming into and out of the project budget at any particular time. If more money is coming in than going out then you have a positive cash flow, if more money is going out than coming in then it is negative. The project budget gives an estimate of the amount of money coming in and going out of the budget each month. Once the project is up and running the actual cash flow is recorded regularly and it may be reported on a monthly basis.

Contract

A contract is a legally enforceable agreement between two parties, e.g. a funding organisation and a recipient organisation. A contract is an agreement for a purchaser to buy a product or service from a supplier, e.g. a funding organisation buys the service of a particular library and information service to deliver a particular project. Contracts are normally written down and signed by both parties, although verbal contracts exist. Those involved in drafting a contract should be very clear about who in their organisation has authority to sign it and ask for clarity from the purchasing or funding organisation if unclear about any terms or conditions. If necessary seek legal advice.

Depreciation

Depreciation is the loss in value of a resource, e.g. a computer. In some financial records it is necessary to include the depreciation of large capital equipment. If a computer is purchased for £5000 and has a life of three years it will depreciate by £1666 per year (value of computer over agreed life period).

Donor, funder or sponsor

The organisation or individual who provides money for projects or other ventures.

Due diligence

Due diligence is the investigation of an organisation to ensure that it is a legitimate business and carries out its activities in a legal and socially responsible manner. In many organisations, the finance or legal teams complete the due diligence process for a potential partner. However, project managers may be involved in providing evidence of due diligence when considering a new partnership.

There are different types of due diligence, relating to commerce, finances, integrity and operations. The outcomes of a due diligence process may include information about the legal status of the organisation; its annual report and financial records; published information about its activities and outputs; and results of an internet search to identify any legal cases or evidence of misconduct, e.g. civil litigation, criminal offences.

Full cost recovery

Full cost recovery means making sure that all project costs and overhead costs are built into the overall cost of a project. All direct project costs such as for staff and equipment used on the project and indirect costs – the overheads that a parent organisation pays such as office space, IT systems, human resources, marketing and public relations – must be included.

Funding stream

A funding stream is the amount of money that has been allocated to a particular initiative or set of initiatives, e.g. e-learning, literacy or digitisation. Funding streams often involve very large amounts of money (millions) over a long time period, e.g. three to five years. The money is released in phases as the programme of work develops.

Grant

A grant is the financial support available from a funding organisation to support a project or other venture. Grants vary in size from £10 to £100 millions. They are often linked to a set of terms and conditions, a contract and/or service level agreement, and if these are not fulfilled the funder may require a repayment of the grant.

Match funding

Match funding takes place when the funding an organisation raises is matched by funding (or non-financial resources) from another organisation, e.g. the organisation receiving the funding. Sometimes, matched funding is received in the form of other resources or services, e.g. volunteer help, gifts in kind such as free office space or furniture, or gifts of service, e.g. legal advice. The value of these resources or services must be calculated and included in project documentation.

Payments

Different funding bodies have different policies and practices with regard to paying the receiving organisation. Block payments occur when the grant is paid in blocks at set stages in the project, e.g. as each milestone is achieved, or at fixed time periods, e.g. every three months. Block payments are the most common method of paying out project funding. There are two other types of payments. Cost and volume payments are made when an agreed volume or amount of service has been achieved; unit pricing or pricing by case occurs when the funder pays an agreed price per unit of provision, e.g. after the delivery of a particular training programme.

Preferred suppliers

Many organisations have a list of preferred suppliers for all who work with them. This often makes the purchasing process easier as these suppliers are already established within the financial systems and are experienced in working with the organisation.

Public–private partnership

A relationship between the public and private sector.

Quotations

A quotation is a written or verbal statement about the cost of a particular job or service. Organisations often require a number of quotations for works, goods or services. For example, if the value of a product or service is less than £4999 there may be no need to obtain a number of quotations. If the value is more than £5000 it may be necessary to obtain a minimum of three quotations. Policies and practices with regard to quotations vary and should be checked.

Service agreement

A service agreement or service level agreement is a contract in which one body agrees to provide a specific service. The service agreement gives details of the required service, e.g. service requirements, performance indicators. It may be between two departments in the same organisation or between different organisations.

Tender

A tender is a written offer to carry out a particular piece of work at a particular price. If the tender is accepted the tenderer is bound to fulfil the offer. Tenders are typically used for large projects, e.g. those valued over £10,000.

Virement

Virement is the process of moving money from one budget heading to another. For example, a project manager may find that she is spending less money than expected on travel and wants to use this money on learning resources – to move (or vire) the money from one budget heading (travel) to another (learning resources). It is essential to obtain permission to vire money, e.g. from the funding body and/or finance manager, in writing.

Bidding and tendering for projects

Experience of the bidding culture suggests that it can be an extremely time-consuming and resource-intensive process. Reading all the relevant paperwork can be heavy going. Writing a succinct bid that meets the needs of the funding organisation as well as the library and information services and its stakeholders can engulf vast swathes of time.

Information workers need expertise or access to expertise in writing bids. Many public sector organisations, for example local authorities and universities, employ specialist staff whose sole remit is keeping up to date with funding organisations and their requirements, and providing help and support in writing bids. This can exclude smaller and independent organisations which may contract the services of a consultant to develop their funding application.

The actual bidding process produces 'winners and losers'. It can be an extremely demoralising experience for individuals and organisations who are unsuccessful in obtaining a bid after they have invested much time and effort. Successful applicants may suddenly find they need to get a project up and running in a matter of weeks, often while still fully engaged in their full-time job.

Although access to external funds provides library and information services with wide-ranging opportunities and the ability to develop new and innovative services, there are disadvantages to working on externally funded projects. For example, they are likely to require specialist reporting and audit regimes, which may cause an administrative burden. The funder may insist on maintaining the timelines in the original project plan even when circumstances have changed, e.g. following delays in recruiting project workers. In addition, the focus of funding is often on outcomes rather than processes, which may put pressure on managers to meet the outcomes at the cost of setting up a sustainable process. The administrative burden of managing the different funding bodies' requirements can be immense for project managers who have obtained funding for their projects from a variety of sources.

The following sections outline the bidding process which is summarised in Figure 8.1.

1. Identify a potential project and starting work on project brief.
2. Identify a potential source of funding.
3. Obtain the necessary documentation.
4. Check funders' requirements and criteria.
5. Check with parent organisation that this meets their aims.
6. Identify and contact a senior manager who will support the funding application.
7. Identify a single individual who will be responsible for the project.
8. Carry out research within the sector.
9. Carry out research within the funding organisation.
10. Attend any briefing meetings hosted by the funding organisation.
11. Establish a bidding team.
12. Produce a draft funding application.
13. Start preparing the supporting documents.
14. Check out queries with the funding organization.
15. Obtain feedback and guidance from colleagues.
16. Edit and re-draft the funding application.
17. Obtain formal approval from own organisation to send off the funding application.
18. Submit the funding application within the timescale identified by the funding organisation.
19. Be prepared to be called to an interview if that is part of the process.
20. Receive outcome of selection process.
21. If successful then rejoicing and starting project. If unsuccessful obtaining feedback from the funding organisation and using it to help you become successful in your next application.

Figure 8.1 *Summary of the bidding process*

Identifying the project

The first stage in bidding for a project is to determine what project to bid for. Many library and information service managers have existing or potential projects that may be used as the focus of a bidding process. These projects may have been identified during the strategic planning process within the library and information service or may have evolved during the day-to-day work within a unit or in response to a particular problem or challenge. It is useful to write down the basic project idea as a project brief (see Chapter 3 for the structure and content of project briefs). It is very important that the brief includes a clear statement of the project's aims and outcomes.

Initial research

The next stage is to identify potential sources of funding and, as suggested earlier in this chapter, this often requires considerable research. Once a potential source of funding is found, obtain the documentation that outlines that organisation's funding programme(s) and requirements. Most funding organisations manage the funding documentation and applications via their website. It is worth monitoring the website at regular intervals so you can pick up any additional information, for example more detailed explanations of their requirements or changes in submission dates.

Once a potential source of funding is identified it is vital to check the details of the funder's requirements to ensure that your project will meet them. Otherwise you may find that you are wasting time preparing a project bid for a funder who would not consider your application. If you are uncertain about a funder's requirements contact the organisation by phone or e-mail. Many funders organise special meetings or briefing sessions for new funding opportunities, which are well worth attending as they give attendees an opportunity to find out more about the funder and what they are looking for. They also provide an opportunity to network with like-minded people and learn from them.

Gaining support
Ensure that the proposed project fits into your organisation's or department's aims and objectives to ensure that if it gains approval your organisation will support the project. As mentioned in Chapter 2, it is vital to gain support for your project from senior managers. Initially 'selling' your idea to one manager is often a good strategy, which can be followed up by ensuring that the project proposal is discussed and (hopefully) supported by the senior team. Identify someone who will take responsibility for putting together the funding application.

Some organisations have a structure with teams of people who will work with you in putting together your bid, advising you on what is required for your application. Other organisations don't have this type of structure and it is helpful to bring together a team of people who will take overall responsibility for the funding application. This team may include the person with overall responsibility for producing the application, individuals who are interested in and enthusiastic about the potential project, technical staff, finance staff and potential project champions.

Preparing the application
The basis of all good funding applications is research, as applicants must demonstrate to the funding organisation that their application is based on

knowledge of current good practice. Many funding applications require you to demonstrate your knowledge of your current context and the ways in which your project will make a difference, so be aware of relevant current government policy and activities within your particular sector (e.g. school library, public library, higher education), area of interest (e.g. digitisation, reading, well-being, information literacy) and across the profession as a whole. This research will enable you to link your application to current thinking and activities, and help you to identify gaps that your project might fill. It will also help you to develop the appropriate language for making the funding application.

Also carry out research on your proposed project within your organisation in order to start thinking through some of the practical aspects of the project. A good starting point is to produce a draft project brief and use it when talking to appropriate colleagues, e.g. the human resource manager, finance director, ICT manager, administrative manager, so you have the appropriate organisational support and understand any policies and practices that you need to implement in the project. Find out what is required to put the project in place. For example, if it takes your organisation three months to recruit a new member of staff this has implications for the project application.

Start preparing the supporting documents required by the funding organisation, for example:

- evidence of the legal status of your organisation
- the annual report
- a set of audited accounts
- selected policies and practices, e.g. diversity policy
- a biography or CV of key people.

Costing

Costing the project is a relatively straightforward activity. Identify all the potential costs of the project. Many organisations have their own set of guidelines and rules for costing projects and it is worth talking to staff in the finance department before you start this activity. Figure 8.2 on the next page provides a list of common costs in library and information service projects.

The major cost in any project is likely to be the staffing. In project work, staff are budgeted for on the basis of their annual salary (pro-rata for part-

People – permanent and contract staff	Consumables
External assistance – consultants, trainers	Stationery
Professional fee, e.g. auditor	Printed materials
Furniture	Hire of meeting rooms
Equipment	Refreshments for meetings
Software	Conference fees
Subscriptions	Travel and subsistence

Figure 8.2 *Common project costs*

time staff) plus on-costs, which are the costs to the organisation of employing someone – items such as employer-related National Insurance costs (in the UK) and pension contributions – and typically 20% of the salary. Some organisations charge an additional overhead for externally funded projects, which may be as much as 20%. It is vital that you know the rules of your organisation before calculating the staff costs. If your project is going to last for more than a year think about including cost of living or performance-related pay rises in your budget.

Consider the number of working days someone is available to actually work on the project. This was discussed in Chapter 4 and the key information is repeated below starting with the calculation on the number of working days available per year.

Working days per year   = Days in year – (annual leave + weekends +
                                          training + statutory days + sick days)
                          = 365 – (20 + 104 + 4 + 11 + 5) days
                          = 221 days per annum

So, as a rough rule of thumb, someone who is working on a project full-time will be available for approximately 221 days' work per year and someone who is spending 50% of their working time on the project will be available for 115.5 days per year. It is important to allocate people on the basis of their actual working days per year otherwise you will seriously underestimate the staffing input required for the project.

In many projects, self-employed librarians, project workers, trainers or consultants are contracted to work for a specified period of time. A daily rate, which may vary from £250 to £1250, is agreed and included in the budget. In the UK, the employing organisation has an obligation to ensure that the individual is self-employed and makes appropriate tax returns.

This normally involves them providing the relevant information and documentation at the contract stage. Again, staff in finance departments can advise.

The other project costs need to be worked out and included in your project budget. An important detail in the UK is whether or not you can claim back VAT on purchases. The rules for VAT are complicated and change over time, so obtain up-to-date specialist advice from your finance department. Another potential issue arises for those working with different currencies as fluctuations in currency exchange can have an adverse or beneficial impact on budgets.

Figure 8.3 presents an example project budget and Figure 8.4 overleaf presents the same budget, demonstrating the intended cash flow over the five-month life of the project. In this example, the indirect costs are calculated at 20% as this is the policy of the parent organisation for developing budgets for externally funded projects. In Figure 8.4, there are two columns (columns 2 and 8) in which the figures are totalled. This provides a useful check on whether or not you have worked out your cash flow carefully.

Estimated expenditure		£
Project manager		25,210
Project worker		15,104
Administrative assistant		1,123
Trainer		1,500
	Subtotal	42,937
ICT		5,000
Hire of training rooms		1,500
Refreshments		240
Marketing and PR		1,500
Attendance at conferences		1,500
Travel and subsistence		250
	Subtotal	9,990
Indirect costs (20% total costs)		8,587
	Total	61,514

Figure 8.3 *Example project budget for a digital skills project*

Estimated expenditure	£	January	February	March	April	May	TOTAL
Project manager	25,210	5,042	5,042	5,042	5,042	5,042	25,210
Project worker	15,104	3,021	3,021	3,021	3,021	3,021	15,104
Administrative assistant	1,123	225	225	225	225	225	1,123
Trainer	1,500			750	750		1,500
Subtotal	42,937						42,937
ICT	5,000	1,500	3,500				5,000
Hire of training rooms	1,500			750	750		1,500
Refreshments	240			120	120		240
Marketing and PR	1,500		800	700			1,500
Attendance at conferences	1,500				350	1,150	1,500
Travel and subsistence	250				55	195	250
Subtotal	9,990						9,990
Indirect costs (20% total costs)	8,587						8,587
Total	61,514						61,514

Figure 8.4 *Example project budget showing estimated expenditure for a digital skills project*

The draft application

The next step is to produce an initial draft funding application, which is a key stage in the funding application process. Circulate the draft application to colleagues (within and external to your organisation) and ask for feedback so it can be worked on and polished until it completely matches the requirements of the funding organisation. Obtaining feedback and guidance from colleagues is an important part of the bidding process as it will help you to sharpen up your application and include a range of ideas and perspectives. It also provides a means of engaging people with the project. Remember that if individuals are generous with their time and experience in helping you to put together your bid it is important to thank them and to repay their work 'in kind' at a later date.

Continue editing the funding application. Keep checking back to the requirements of the funding organisation to ensure that your application does not drift and develop in new directions (that don't meet the requirements of the funding organisation) as time goes by. This is a lengthy process; draft applications go through many iterations before they are ready for submission. Take any questions or issues that arise during this feedback process and meetings of the bidding team to the funding organisation. The more clarity you have about the funding organisation's expectations the more likely you are to meet them.

Submitting the application

Once the funding application is ready obtain approval from your manager and/or organisation to send it off. Many funding organisations require that the funding application is supported by a statement of commitment from a senior member of staff, for example the director of the library service, the head teacher, or a director of the organisation. It is vital that you submit the funding application within the timescale specified by the funding organisation. This sounds obvious, but many large national or international funding organisations will not consider an application if it is one second late. If you are submitting your application electronically it is always a good idea to submit it at least 24 hours before the closing date and time, in case you need to sort out any unexpected technical difficulties. Keep the receipt or acknowledgement that you delivered your application.

Some funding bodies include an interview at the shortlisting stage so be prepared to be called to one. These often involve a brief presentation followed by a question and answer session. It can be useful to bring a senior colleague with you to demonstrate you have institutional support for the project. Presentations are considered in Chapter 6.

Outcomes of your application

Different funding organisations inform applicants of the outcome of applications over different timescales and by different means, for example by phone, e-mail or letter. This information should be provided in the details about their requirements. It is best practice not to contact a funding organisation until after the deadline for informing applicants about the results of the bidding process has passed. Numerous phone calls from worried applicants before this deadline are a source of great irritation and a time-waster for funding organisations.

Remember to inform colleagues and stakeholders of the results of your application for funding, and thank those who contributed to it, whether successful or not. If it is successful you are likely to move into the project-planning or implementation stage of the project (see Chapters 4 and 5).

Many project applications are unsuccessful and it is worth obtaining feedback from the funding organisation, if rejected to learn from the experience and, hopefully, make it more likely that your next funding application will be successful.

More detailed information and advice on bids, tenders and proposals is available in Lewis (2015).

Crowdfunding

Crowdfunding is the practice of funding a venture by asking the public for financial support in the form of donations via a crowdfunding site such as Indiegogo, Kickstarter, Razoo, CauseVox and Fundly, which takes a percentage of the donations to pay for their costs. It is becoming an increasingly common approach for libraries to access alternative funding.

Case study 8.1   The introduction of a nine-foot tall Incredible Hulk statue in a public library

The Northlake public library near Chicago launched a fundraising appeal on Indiegogo asking readers to donate money to help them buy a Hulk statue, graphic novels and a 'creation station' that would enable users to create their own comics and films. They achieved their target (approximately £20,000) and obtained the statue for the library. Depending on the amount they donated, donors were offered a range of rewards or options including a 'get-out-of-fines' card, a postcard in which a librarian dressed up as a comic character and held a speech bubble with a personalised message, to a picture on a plaque in the library, a Hulk library card and a picture of the Hulk holding the plaque. This creative and imaginative activity helped to generate money as well as world-wide publicity, and proved popular with customers (see https://www.indiegogo.com/projects/bring-the-hulk-to-the-northlake-public-library).

Crowdfunding by libraries and information services is most successful when the library has a strong social media presence.

Crowdfunding in libraries often involves requesting relatively small amounts of money, e.g. £500–1000, for purposes such as:

- buying new stock
- restoring and preserving particular items
- employing an author or poet in residence.

Here is some general guidance on establishing a crowdfunding project:

- Find out what the approach of your library and information service or parent organisation is to crowdfunding. Is there a policy? From whom do you need to obtain formal permission for your proposed campaign?
- Research your project and audience. Consider your project and whether or not it is likely to appeal to a wide audience. How much funding do you require? Consider your social media presence – do you have a large following?
- Research crowdfunding. Identify and follow some crowdfunding campaigns. Identify what appears to work and generate interest.
- Find out which crowdfunding host site is suitable for your type of project. Read the terms of use of several host sites, note their fees and the percentage of the donations they take. Does the site provide analytics so you can monitor the progress of your campaign? Will the site enable you to provide links to and from your library and information service?
- Think about your crowdfunding campaign. How will you keep it live? Will you be able to recruit colleagues or volunteers to help promote it? How can you use all your contacts and networks to help make it a vigorous campaign? Think beyond social media, e.g. to newspapers, TV and radio.
- Think about the length of time needed for your campaign. Normally they last 30–90 days although emergency campaigns are shorter – up to 30 days. How much time will you be able to put into the campaign during this period?
- Develop a crowdfunding case that is succinct, appealing and convincing. Can you provide a range of images, videos or stories to support your campaign?
- Think about the project management of a crowdfunding appeal. Who will manage the project? Use project management tools and techniques to manage your crowdfunding project professionally.

Managing the finances

Once you have obtained agreement to go ahead with the project and the budget you will need to manage the finances and keep appropriate records. The best starting point is to ask advice from a finance officer in your organisation or the funding organisation. They will advise you on how to keep records of your project's income and expenditure, and the importance of keeping a record of all transactions. Normally, all records are kept on the finance system of your organisation and it is worth spending time with the accounts staff to make sure that you understand and use the system properly.

When I have been a project manager, I have always kept my own record of income and expenditure on a spreadsheet as this enables me to see the project finances at a glance. Although this practice was never popular with the finance team, it helped me to diagnose differences between my records and those on the financial system, particularly if information had gone astray or been miscoded.

Once the project starts monitor project costs carefully. This is most easily managed using a spreadsheet and updating it regularly. Keep a cumulative report, which shows the budgeted and actual costs (sometimes called a variance report). This is demonstrated in Figure 8.5, which only illustrates the actual costs for the first month of the project (owing to space constraints).

Estimated expenditure (£)		January		Variance (£)
	£	Budget (£)	Actual (£)	
Project manager	25,210	5,042	2,021	3,021
Project worker	15,104	3,021	3,021	0
Administrative assistant	1,123	225	113	112
Trainer	1,500			
Subtotal	42,937			
ICT	5,000	1,500	1,700	- 200
Hire of training rooms	1,500			
Refreshments	240			
Marketing and PR	1,500			
Attendance at conferences	1,500			
Travel and subsistence	250			
Subtotal	9,990			
Indirect costs (20% total costs)	8,587			
Total	61,514			
Variance				2,933

Figure 8.5 *Example spreadsheet showing actual costs and variance for a digital skills project*

In reality, you would work with a spreadsheet set up for the whole life of the project – a version of Figure 8.5 with the added columns for actual expenditure and variance each month. The variance is the difference between the budgeted costs, which were estimates, and the actual costs. If the variance is positive (shown by a + sign) your spending is under-budget. If the variance is negative (shown by a − sign) your spending is over-budget and you need to take appropriate action. Project managers are normally required to provide summary reports at regular intervals, e.g. for the project management or steering group, and/or the funding body. A common issue with many project budgets is that the projected or planned budget does not match the reality of running the project. Estimates of expenditure may be different from the actual expenditure. Some items may be more expensive and others cheaper than anticipated in the budget. Sometimes, it is possible to sort out these differences by transferring money from one budget heading to another, e.g. from a travel heading to a conference heading. In this situation, contact either the finance officer or the funding body and ask for permission to vire or transfer the funding from one heading to another. Most funding organisations are experienced in project management and know that budgets often have to be adapted once the project has started to be implemented. It is vital that you obtain written approval of changes of this kind for audit purposes.

If a project goes over their budget this should be reported to the steering group and senior manager responsible for the project as soon as it becomes apparent, as they may decide to discontinue it.

Being prepared and taking part in audits

Many funding bodies require as part of the contract that the recipient of their funds obtains an auditor's report to demonstrate that they have properly accounted for their funds. In most cases, the finance department of the host organisation of the library and information service can recommend an auditor and help to support the auditing process. In some cases funding organisations send in their own auditors. Internally funded projects may also be audited, e.g. as part of the normal financial processes of that organisation. As project manager, if you have any input into who will be carrying out the audit it is normally best to choose an auditor with experience of auditing similar projects.

It is good practice to be prepared for a potential audit from the very start of the project. Keep accurate records and copies (either digital or print-based) of all records, e.g. receipts and invoices. The auditor normally checks all the project financial records, including contracts, payroll details, invoices and receipts, as well as any formal notices, e.g. agreeing to the virement of funds from one budget heading to another. The auditor ensures that all the money is properly accounted for and that there is an audit trail that demonstrates how every penny has been spent. The more carefully you keep records during the life of the project the easier it will be to prepare for and respond to the audit.

Summary

This chapter gave an insight into the important area of project finances and includes a summary of technical terms. It considers project funding and the process of obtaining funds from external organisations by formally submitting a bid. There is an introduction to crowdfunding and using this to resource a project.

Project managers are normally required to manage a budget, which may be audited. Again, practical advice is provided on these essential aspects of managing the finances of a project. An important message in this chapter is to obtain advice from your organisation's finance team as early as possible in the life of the project.

References and further reading

De Farber, B. G. (2016) *Collaborative Grant-Seeking: a practical guide for librarians*, Rowman and Littlefield Publishers.

Hallam, A. W. and Dalston, T. R. (2004) *Managing Budgets and Finances: a how-to-do-it manual for librarians and information professionals*, Neal-Schuman Publishers.

Hall-Ellis, S., Bowers, S. and Hudson, C. (2011) *Librarian's Handbook for Seeking, Writing, and Managing Grants*, Libraries Unlimited.

Lewis, H. (2015) *Bids, Tenders and Proposals*, Kogan Page.

Smallwood, C. (editor) (2011) *The Frugal Librarian: thriving in tough economic times*, American Library Association.

Turner, A. M. (2007) *Managing Money: a guide for librarians*, McFarland and Co.

CHAPTER 9

The people side of projects

Introduction

This chapter explores the people side of projects. Library and information workers regularly find themselves working in a variety of teams ranging from small in-house teams through to multi-professional and collaborative teams made up of workers from a variety of professions and organisations. The project team may include staff on permanent contracts as well as those recruited specifically for the project on temporary contracts. Virtual teams may involve people working on the same project from across the world, working across time zones and geographical boundaries. Many library and information services now support projects that work with volunteers, particularly on special projects and through crowdsourcing.

This chapter discusses fundamental requirements for project workers, developing working practices, working in diverse teams, working in virtual teams, working with volunteers, crowdsourcing and the management of change.

Fundamental requirements for project workers

It is vital that short-term contract staff working on a project are given an appropriate working environment and access to services. This may appear obvious but I have worked in a number of organisations where this did not occur and contract staff received a poor introduction to the project and organisation. The basic requirements of contract staff is to have:

- access to an appropriate working environment, e.g. desk, ICT, telephone
- an introduction to key people within the organisation, library and information service, and the project
- an induction process that provides information about:
  – the organisation and information and library service

- organisational policies and working practices on health and safety, use of ICT and social media, the bullying and harassment policy, and so on
- human resource practices on contracts, payroll and pensions, policies and procedures relating to annual and sick leave, perform-ance management and appraisal processes, and staff and career development
- the project: its history and progress, working practices and key issues.

If there is space consider providing special project space to colleagues working on the project as part of their normal working life so they can get away from the demands of their everyday work and focus 100% on the project for periods of time. This helps them not to be torn between the demands of the project and their other work.

Case study 9.1   An isolated project worker

I worked for a very short time on a university-based retrospective catalogue conversion project. At the start of my contract, the induction process took about 15 minutes and I discovered that my 'office' was a desk in the corner of a book store. This was in an isolated area of the library and only very occasionally visited by other library staff seeking items in this store. As a result, I rarely had contact with others. At my monthly meetings with my line manager we focused completely on the tasks in hand and whether or not targets had been met. At no time was there any discussion about my experiences on the project, my staff development needs or my career after the project concluded. I became very unhappy and decided to find another job, left the project as quickly as possible and moved on to another role. The project manager had to find and train another project worker who also left the project after a very short time.

Case study 9.2   Hot desking

Agata was employed on a one-year contract to help develop the library and information website and social media in a public library in London. On her first day, her manager greeted her and explained that, apart from her first week, she would be hot desking like the rest of the staff. The hot desking area was used by a range of staff, including people from other teams, e.g. customer services and ICT. She was shown a locker where she would keep her personal belongings. Agata enjoyed her first week's work and thought that the induction process had worked well and that she was beginning to meet the team. However, she found the hot desking aspect of her working life challenging as she constantly moved between two floors in the building and found it difficult to build working relationships with colleagues as she was always sitting near different people.

Over time Agata got used to this way of working and soon learnt that if she got to work very early she had a choice of desks and could choose one that she liked. She also appreciated that it enabled her to get to know a wider range of colleagues than if she was located in one office. This helped her to improve her knowledge of the organisation. However, after the end of the contract, she moved to another role in another public library and was keen to have a permanent desk.

Developing working practices

It is well worth project managers thinking about the culture and working practices they want to develop within the team. The initial team meeting is extremely important as it sets the tone for the whole project, so it should be organised in such a way that team members feel welcome and encouraged to think that the whole project experience is going to be positive. Factors that can help oil the process include giving clear instructions about the meeting and travel arrangements, and providing refreshments on arrival. The agenda of this meeting is likely to include:

- introductions
- an outline of the project brief
- areas of concern: hopes, fears and expectations
- project aims, outcomes and milestones
- project management and governance
- project team: roles and responsibilities
- project processes: ground rules and working practices
- questions and answers
- an outline action plan.

This initial meeting is all about getting to know each other and the proposed project. The project brief provides a useful starting point to ensuring that everyone understands the project and its boundaries. The meeting is also about identifying and agreeing working practices. A useful way of establishing team member and project manager responsibilities is to ask the meeting to split into sub-groups and for each group to list the responsibilities of team members and the project manager. These can be shared and written up. The final list can then be used as an informal contract for the project team and circulated as part of the notes from the meeting. The project manager may find it useful to use this list when inducting late arriving team members or revising it if colleagues don't fulfil their responsibilities. It is important to use the actual language that is used in the meeting rather than to tidy it up and make it into a formal document, which would be different from the one agreed by the team. Table 9.1 shows the suggestions made by colleagues when I carried out this activity at the start of a project.

Table 9.1 *Responsibilities of team members and project managers*

Team member	Project manager
To keep their promises	To be honest and open about the project
To keep deadlines	To keep the team fully informed about good and bad project news
To be honest about progress and share good and bad news as soon as possible	To report back from meetings with senior managers
To support each other and the project manager	To keep the team informed of all developments
To manage their time	To give positive feedback and support the team
To reply to e-mails within 48 hours	To be available to the project team in person and via e-mail (all replies within 48 hours)

It is worth spending some time at the first meeting to let people air any concerns, fears or unhappiness about the project. One way of managing this process is to ask the team to work in small groups of three or four, and to identify their 'hopes and fears' about the project. They can feed back to the whole group. In the feedback process it is important to ask for the 'fears' first as this will raise any negative issues. Once these have been dealt with move on to the 'hopes', so you end up on a positive note. If necessary set a time limit on the feedback process or limit each group to two fears and two hopes. This helps to prevent the whole process being swamped by potential negativity. At this stage it is worth mentioning that the majority of project teams are made up of positive and constructive staff!

Managing a project team involves focusing on and working with individuals, the team and the task. As project manager you will need to know the individual team members and their strengths and weaknesses. You will decide the action plan, give information to and receive feedback from team members through e-mails, text messages or phone calls, and help and support them as required. Motivation is important in team work and you may be required to spend some time encouraging and supporting staff.

All project workers, whether working on contracts or carrying out project work as part of their 'normal' library and information role, should be able to work as effective team members. Informal discussions with participants on project management workshops identify the following qualities of effective project team members:

- being punctual
- communicating clearly and honestly
- communicating regularly, e.g. by e-mail
- exchanging information
- being flexible
- contributing their share of the workload
- identifying problems (and come up with potential solutions)
- giving and asking for help
- giving constructive feedback
- keeping their promises
- meeting deadlines.

The main barriers to effective project team work are often caused by individuals who:

- talk down the project
- are cynical about the project and its potential value
- complain and moan about the project, project manager or project team
- 'disappear', e.g. go on holiday without informing the project manager or other colleagues
- don't respond to e-mails, text or phone messages
- don't keep their promises and deliver their work on time
- keep vital information to themselves
- are not prepared to be flexible and help other team members who may be struggling

- moan about their workload
- arrange to be away from work during critical times of the project.

It is helpful to start a project with a meeting where you decide and record your agreed working practices. If anyone puts up any of the barriers to teamwork listed above, sit down in a private meeting with them, and discuss their behaviour with reference to the team's agreed working practices.

In any project that involves people working together there are likely to be some disagreements and conflict. Common problems that arise in project and team work include individuals not pulling their weight, someone not sharing information, disagreement about a particular decision, people wasting time, having too much work, confusion and/or personality clashes. The ability to reach agreement and resolve conflict is an important part of effective team working. Deal effectively with any problems that arise in a team as the consequences of not doing so may be that you fail to meet your goal. This could lead to repercussions such as the library and information service losing a client, a contract, money and its reputation; the team losing credibility or power, or being disbanded; and/or individuals being blamed, achieving poor appraisal results or even losing their jobs.

Conflicts and disagreements can be tackled through:

- *competition* – the creation of win–lose situations, which is likely to result in the 'losers' feeling aggrieved and possibly losing their motivation for the project
- *avoidance* – where the conflict is ignored in the hope that it will go away; they tend to grow rather than disappear
- *compromise* – where the individuals concerned each find a way of giving up something while gaining part of what they require
- *consensus* – where discussions take place until everyone agrees on a particular course of action
- *collaboration* – where a solution is found that satisfies everyone's requirements
- *accommodation* – where one or more people put the needs of another above their own needs.

Competition and avoidance are not particularly effective ways of dealing with conflict or disagreement. Ideally, the project manager and team need to find a way of compromising, reaching consensus, collaboration or accommodation over the issue.

There are many different approaches to managing conflict; one useful strategy is to follow the following five steps:

1 Identify the source of conflict.
2 Understand each person's position.
3 Define the problem.
4 Search for and evaluate alternative solutions.
5 Agree upon and implement the best solution.

The first step is to analyse the situation and identify the source of conflict. This may be an obvious source or it may be an indirect one. The next step is to give everyone a chance to have their say. Let them report the facts of the situation. They will also need to share their feelings. Listen to what they have to say. Remember to read their body language too. Using the information you have gained from the second step to define the problem. Summarise the situation as you see it. Check that everyone agrees with your definition. As a team, look for alternative solutions. You may want to ask for assistance, for example from a critical friend. Once you have obtained a number of potential solutions then evaluate them, e.g. by listing their advantages and disadvantages. As a team, agree the best solution. Make sure that everyone agrees positively and that their verbal and non-verbal language are congruent. If anyone looks unhappy with the solution then discuss it with them. Once everyone is in total agreement implement the best solution.

Further reading on managing teams includes: Brent, M. and Dent, F. (2013) *The Leader's Guide to Managing People: how to use soft skills to get hard results*, FT Publishing; Hawkins, P. (2014), *Leadership Team Coaching*, Kogan Page; Wellington, P. (2012) *Managing Successful Teams*, Kogan Page.

Working with diverse teams

As with much library and information work, project work frequently involves working together with people from a range of cultures: different organisational cultures, countries and perhaps generations. Culture is extremely deep-rooted and includes unconscious values, for example about ways of behaving with other people, different practices in such matters as rituals, heroes and symbols, and different ways of being. The following paragraphs describe Hofstede's (1994) research on cultures and organisations, which has stood the test of time and provides a useful framework for thinking about working in diverse teams.

Hofstede (1994) identifies six layers of culture: country level (where we live or have lived); regional, ethnic, religious and/or linguistic affiliation level; gender level; generation level, e.g. teenagers, young professionals, over 70s; social-class level associated with educational opportunities, occupation or profession; and finally organisational or corporate level (for those who are employed). Hofstede suggested there are five cultural dimensions that project managers need to take into account when they are working across national boundaries:

- *Individualism* – the extent to which people think of themselves as individuals or members of a group. In individualistic countries such as Canada, France and Germany people are expected to look after themselves and having personal time, freedom and challenges are important values. This is in contrast to collectivist cultures such as Greece, Japan and South Korea where individuals are bonded through strong relationship ties based on loyalty to a group such as the family, team or employer, and the team or group is considered more important than the individual.
- *Power distance* – the distance between managers and workers and the importance of hierarchy. In high-power-distance countries such as Latin America and many Asian and African countries, workers tend to be afraid of their managers and leaders (who tend to be paternalistic and autocratic) and treat them with respect. In contrast in low-power-distance countries (such as the UK, the USA and most of Europe) workers are more likely to challenge their managers (who tend to use a consultative management style).
- *Gender* – the extent to which feminine values are treated equally to masculine values. In countries such as Hong Kong, Japan, the UK and the USA, where the masculinity index is high, people tend to value challenging work, opportunities for gaining a high income, personal recognition for their work, and opportunities for advancement to a higher-level job. In countries such as Denmark, France, Israel and Sweden, where feminine values are given greater prominence than elsewhere, people tend to value good working relationships, co-operative behaviours and long-term job security.

- *Certainty dimension* – the extent to which people prefer unstructured and unpredictable environments rather than structured and predictable ones. People in cultures with a strong uncertainty dimension such as Japan and South Korea tend to avoid unknown situations which they perceive to be threatening. In contrast in countries such as Hong Kong, the Netherlands, Singapore, the UK and the USA where uncertainty avoidance is weak, people feel less threatened by unknown situations. They are also more likely to be open to innovations, risk and so on.
- *Time orientation* – the extent to which people prefer a long-term or a short-term time orientation. People in countries such as China, Hong Kong, Japan and Taiwan demonstrate a long-term time orientation characterized by persistence, perseverance, respect for a hierarchy of the status of relationships, thrift and a sense of shame. In contrast people in countries such as Australia, Canada, Germany and the UK have a short-term orientation, marked by a sense of security and stability, a protection of one's reputation, a respect for tradition and a reciprocation of favours.

As with any model, this perhaps over-simplifies culture but it does provide useful information on the potential behaviour of individuals from different cultures. The implications of this model for project managers or information workers is to be aware that their teams are made up of a diverse group of people who are likely to have different approaches to their work.

Individuals experienced in working within a collectivist culture are likely to find themselves on familiar territory with collaborative team work but may feel exposed if asked to work in an extremely individualistic manner. In contrast, a team that is predominately made up of information workers from countries with a low-power distance may inadvertently exclude a team worker from a high-power-distance country who is not familiar or comfortable with the rest of their team's relationship with their manager, including being prepared to challenge her. At the same time, a project manager may enjoy working with uncertainty and ambiguity during the project process and find it frustrating that workers from elsewhere, for example from cultures with a strong uncertainty dimension, want high levels of structure imposed on the project.

Hofstede's work is useful as it reminds us that different people have different needs and work and relate to each other in very different ways.

However it is important to avoid using this type of categorisation to stereotype and label people: individuals within a culture are extremely diverse too. The key message for project managers is to get to know your team and the individuals within it. You will then be able to adapt your management style to take into account and be sensitive to the different concerns of individual team workers: their caring responsibilities, desire to attend faith festivals, approaches to food or drink, and so on.

Working with virtual teams

Frequently, library and information workers are involved in projects that work across national boundaries and time zones in virtual teams using e-mail, messaging, tools such as Skype or FaceTime, project management software or video conferencing to communicate. Many of these tools are discussed in Chapter 7. Some project teams never meet face to face while others may meet once or twice during the life of the project.

As long as the technology works it provides individual team members with the opportunity to engage fully with the project from their desktop at a time and place that suits them, but it also raises some challenges to team work. How do you develop trust and confidence in a team and its members if you have never met them? How do you manage a project team whom you have never met? How do you take into account the different cultural backgrounds of information workers from a wide range of countries?

Working together in face-to-face teams gives individuals the opportunity to size each other up, get to know each other's work style, habits and preferences, and build relationships. In particular, sitting around a meeting table enables you to gain very quick feedback from someone's replies (or silences) and their body language. In contrast, virtual team working involves communicating with other team members through text with or without visual images. Yet individuals need to get to know each other and develop trust in their project manager and team members.

In virtual teams, the role of the project manager includes managing technical, project and social aspects of the communications process.

When managing technical aspects of the communications process ensure:

- there is an appropriate virtual communication platform
- there is appropriate technical support
- that the administrative arrangements, e.g. user IDs and passwords, are in place.

When managing project aspects of the communications process:

- manage the project work overall
- monitor and control tasks and activities
- provide feedback and support to individuals and group(s)
- offer advice and support to those with problems.

When managing social aspects of the communications process develop:

- an appropriate online working environment
- friendly informal communications.

Case study 9.3   Collaborative project with members in the UK and China

Janine is a liaison librarian working in a UK university, which has partners in a number of countries, including China. The university is establishing a new partnership in China and she is the lead person from library and learning resources. The small project team of two librarians from each university chiefly communicate through e-mail and Skype, and this works well. However, the difference in the time zone is that China is eight hours ahead of the UK, so they schedule meetings between 8 a.m. and 10 a.m. UK time.

In an informal conversation, Janine reported that the partnership worked well and that the more they got to know each other, the easier it was to work together. She valued learning about Chinese culture, e.g. the importance of the Chinese New Year and the holiday taken by the librarians at this time, and the working life of librarians in China. She said that there were occasional miscommunications but they rarely interrupted the project work as all partners took time to double check their understanding of each other's messages.

Case study 9.4   Collaborative project with members in England and Saudi Arabia

Peter had completed a doctorate in information science and during his studies made friends with a student who was a librarian in Saudi Arabia. After the end of their studies, they decided to collaborate on a joint paper for publication in a peer-reviewed journal. Originally they wanted to hold discussions via Skype or FaceTime, but found out that there were difficulties gaining access to Skype and FaceTime (and equivalent systems) in Saudi Arabia so relied wholly on e-mail. Peter said that this was not a problem – they had built up a good relationship

> when they were students together, which helped them to understand each other's style of working. They were very pleased when the paper was accepted for publication with only minor revisions.

These are some practical tips for virtual team work:

- Ask everyone to post a brief biography with a photograph.
- Check out the difference in time zones. Arrange virtual meetings at different times so that team members take turns when there are early or late sessions. Buy some extra clocks, label them and set them to the times of the different countries where your team members are located.
- Check out the annual holidays and festivals of each county, include them in the project diary, and send each other appropriate greetings at these times.
- Agree working practices for your virtual project team, e.g. over attendance at virtual meetings, response times to e-mails.
- Agree ground rules for virtual project meetings, e.g. turn off mobile phones, one person contributes at a time.
- Include time for relationship building at the beginning and end of each online meeting. This allows you to compensate for a lack of the informal communications that take place when team workers are co-located.
- Create time for 'chat'. Some project managers arrange online parties and lunches (everyone brings their own lunch but eat and chat together using virtual communication tools).
- Acknowledge and respect cultural diversity.
- If possible augment virtual activities with face-to-face meetings.
- Hold review meetings to reflect on the process of virtual team working and how it may be improved.

Further reading on virtual teams includes: Lepsinger, R. and DeRosa, D (2010) *Virtual Team Success: A Practical Guide for Working and Leading from a Distance*, Jossey Bass; Pullman, P. (2016) *Virtual Leadership*, Kogan Page.

Working with volunteers

Many library and information services work with volunteers who may be involved in supporting special projects or events, as well as the everyday working life of the project. Volunteers are often willing to give their time and energy to specific projects or libraries to develop their knowledge and skills, meet new people and be part of a team, giving something back to the community, and/or because they believe in the goal or purpose of the project. Volunteers bring a number of benefits: energy, enthusiasm and ideas; sharing the workload; and facilitating the engagement of the wider community.

When working with volunteers think about:

- the reason you want to involve volunteers
- the role and responsibilities of the volunteers
- the amount of time volunteers may commit to the project
- the ways in which volunteers will work with the paid staff
- payment of expenses, e.g. travel to and from the project site
- how volunteers will be supported
- their recruitment and selection:
  - how to advertise volunteering roles
  - how to encourage a diverse range of applicants and make them welcome
  - how to respond to enquiries
  - what information you provide to potential volunteers
  - what information you require from volunteers
  - whether you need a screening process and, for example, in the UK Disclosure and Barring Checks (essential for anyone who will have contact with people under the age of 18 and vulnerable adults)
  - how to verify applications, e.g. by asking for references
  - how to inform volunteers of their success or otherwise
- their induction and training, including to:
  - key people
  - the organisation and library and information service
  - relevant policies and practices, such as health and safety, diversity and inclusion, and safeguarding
  - the project and their role in it
  - their specific tasks
- where they will work
- working practices, including teamwork, feedback and support

- how they will be supported and managed
- how you review your experience of working with volunteers.

Finally, it is worth remembering that volunteers are unpaid. They are giving their time and energy for free, so they should not be asked to go through complex recruitment processes, e.g. fill in long application forms, or experience terrifying interview processes. Keep it low key and friendly: talk about coming in for a chat rather than attending an interview. Keep in touch with them while they are volunteering on the project and remember to thank them.

Case study 9.5   Hull City of Culture 2017

I decided to volunteer for the Hull City of Culture 2017 as I knew it would provide me with a wide range of opportunities to engage with events and activities taking place in the libraries (public, school and university), museums and art galleries. A friend had become a volunteer and she was very enthusiastic about the whole programme. This encouraged me to sign up which I did online responding to a series of questions about myself and my experiences.

Soon I was informed by e-mail that I would be invited to an interview when the organisers were dealing with their next cohort of volunteers. This interview took place a month later and was a very relaxed event, at which the concept of the City of Culture and my application were discussed, and I had an opportunity to ask questions. Then I was asked to try on and select the correct size of a volunteer's uniform.

Three weeks after the interview, I was informed that I had been successful and was invited to two mandatory training events. The first was all about the City of Culture and its programme, concluding with a pub-style quiz about the city. The second was an orientation, being given information about Hull 2017 volunteers, training opportunities, how to sign up for volunteering shifts, working on volunteering shifts, safeguarding, online support tools, the uniform, and a volunteer checklist. By the end of the session I had met other volunteers, understood how the Hull 2017 volunteering programme worked, and had a well written and accessible guide to volunteering for the Hull City of Culture 2017. Three weeks later, I collected my uniform and started signing up for shifts.

During the year, I had the opportunity to take part in a wide range of events from supporting the information hub in the railway station through to guiding people in the Ferens Art Gallery, providing information and advice at outdoor art installations, and supporting events in the local university and public libraries. In addition, I had access to a wonderful range of training events, on subjects ranging from water safety through to the history of Hull. It was a great experience and enabled me to learn more about art and culture, meet a wide range of new people, and help support the transformation of Hull.

My reflection on my experience as a volunteer is that the actual recruitment and selection process seemed to take a long time but it prepared me very well for working as a volunteer. I also appreciated that as the programme had more than 4000 volunteers the staff needed a highly structured process to support and manage us. However, once I had completed the recruitment process I had a great time.

Crowdsourcing

Crowdsourcing is the process of obtaining information, services or other inputs, e.g. resources, from the public. It is often used in library and information services in projects relating to family history, local history, or an individual or event. The use of volunteers to help develop and support collections is not new, but crowdsourcing provides a chance for a potentially world-wide audience to engage with the work of libraries, information services and archives. Crowdsourcing is typically managed via the internet, for example a project team manager might make an open call for information or resources, e.g. photographs.

Van Hyning (2016) writes about using crowdsourcing to enrich collections and develop relationships with the public. She describes the use of the research crowdsourcing platform, Zooniverse, which hosts over 50 projects in a wide range of subjects. Example projects include Operation War Diary (https://www.operationwardiary.org), which is concerned with transcribing and tagging diaries; Notes from Nature (https://www.notesfromnature. org), which enables participants to help transform the written word into an online resource; and Emigrant City (http://emigrantcity.nypl.org), which transcribes and indexes more than 6000 mortgage records, to be used by researchers in the humanities and family historians.

Van Hyning (2016) describes the work of Zooniverse as follows:

All bespoke Zooniverse projects, including those built on the free project builder, have a few core components that differentiate them and the platform as a whole from other crowdsourcing projects and platforms. Each image, audio or video file (data point) is independently assessed by multiple individuals, whose responses are then aggregated using a variety of algorithms to determine what is in a given image. With relatively quick tasks, such as animal identification in Snapshot Serengeti, upwards of 70 people will see each image, whereas with more complex text transcription tasks, three to 10 people will do each line or page (depending on the project). Studies have found that non-expert classifiers are nearly as good as experts, with Zooniverse data used in well over 100 publications. All projects have an object-oriented discussion forum called Talk. Here volunteers can ask questions, interact with researchers and fellow volunteers, create their own 'collections', and use hashtags to group together areas of interest.

Case study 9.6   Crowdsourcing at the British Library

The British Library, in association with BL Labs, provides a platform for hosting experimental crowdsourcing projects, which is aimed at improving access to the libraries collections. Examples include:

- Pinyin Card Catalogue: Drawer Five, which enables individuals to help transform printed cards to electronic records for their online catalogue
- Lord Chamberlain's Plays (LCP): 1824–99 (Abbe-Belles), which helps to create a catalogue of Lord Chamberlain's plays and correspondence
- Urdu Card Catalogue: Drawer Two, focused on transforming a printed card catalogue into an online database.

These projects all demonstrate the following characteristics:

- a very clear focus
- simple instructions
- general feedback, e.g. beside every project is information about the percentage completed, number of tasks remaining, number of volunteers working on the project, and how long ago someone was active on the project
- feedback to volunteers, e.g. visual images showing the most active volunteers.

These projects from the British Library can be viewed at: https://www.libcrowds.com.

Case study 9.7   Trove at the National Library of Australia

The National Library of Australia uses crowdsourcing to annotate and correct scanned newspaper text in its collections. This project is known as Trove (http://trove.nla.gov.au) and the website is well worth visiting. Statistics displayed on the website for 22 February 2017 were:

- 8,185 newspaper text corrections today
- 2,675 images from users this month
- 13,579 items tagged this week
- 4,178 comments added this month
- 391 works merged or split this month
- 797 lists this month.

These figures demonstrate the work of thousands of volunteers in supporting Trove. The website and user interface are friendly and accessible. There are many sources of support including a very active online discussion group.

The basic project management tools and techniques described earlier in this book are used when running a crowdsourcing project. Here is some additional guidance for developing and running one:

- Select a very focused and specific project that is attractive to participants.
- Think through what you would like the volunteers to do.
- Work out the estimated duration for the project.
- Work out the detailed task(s) that you want carried out.
- Keep it simple.
- Use a flow chart.
- Pilot your instructions with colleagues, family and friends.
- Identify how you will recruit and support volunteers.
- Identify and select an appropriate crowdsourcing host site.
- Develop an online system using your crowdsourcing host that provides:
  - welcome information
  - simple guidance on the task
  - feedback mechanisms, e.g. the number of tasks completed, the number of people involved, individual feedback when milestones are achieved, e.g. first 10, 50, 100 items
  - encouragement and motivation
  - the use of blogs, videos or other media

- the use of badges, certificates or other 'rewards'
- online help and support.
- Develop an online community by supporting online teams (with team leaders), discussion groups and an occasional webinar.
- Identify how you will manage project closure.

Managing change

All project work involves change. The introduction and implementation of strategic projects result in major changes within the library and information service. Examples of strategic projects include the merger of two libraries, the merger of a library service and an IT service, the restructuring of a service, or a change in direction, e.g. from a public service to a self-funding service. These types of major change have a big impact on library and information service staff as well as the stakeholders. For example, some individuals may feel that they joined and committed themselves to one library service or approach to work, and that this is now being fundamentally challenged and changed. This affects their professional identity and they may feel stressed and challenged. Consequently, if you are involved in project managing strategic change in addition to your other project management tasks, also consider your approach to managing change.

Case study 9.8   Merging two services

I was involved in merging a library service and an ICT service in a university in the north of England. It was a strategic project whose overall aim was to improve the student experience and streamline help desk services. The service was delivered in six buildings (on three campuses) in a city and two buildings (on one campus) in a town 50 miles away. It took more than two hours to travel between the city and the town so staff only made the journey when it was essential. Consequently, the team at the somewhat remote town were less well integrated into the service than other staff.

As a manager within the service, I visited the campus at the more remote town at least once a month and more often during the change process. I held a number of meetings with the library and ICT staff in this campus and talked through how changes would affect them and their customers. My approach was one of collaboration as I explained the framework that we were working in, and I asked staff to work together to develop the detail so that it would fit the local environment. Overall, the atmosphere was a little tense but constructive.

A few months into the project, colleagues were talking about the need to re-arrange their working space so that library and ICT staff had desks near to the service points. This entailed a major move of desks. I said that it was up to them and their team leaders how they organised their working space and left it to them to sort out. A week later when I was at the campus, one of the library staff asked to see me. She was in a rage and said, 'I have been working here for 13 years and I don't see why I should move my desk after all this time. All I want to do is the same job with the same team. I am a library assistant and I want to stick to my original job description and desk.'

I was quite taken aback by this outburst as the assistant had been quiet in all the team meetings and her body language appeared neutral. It made me realise that there was a lot to do when supporting the change process and team leaders. It also helped me to see the value of the change cycle, which is described next.

Figure 9.1 presents a cycle that is commonly used to describe the stages someone goes through as they experience change. The first stage is shock. Individuals may literally be shocked, feel numb, helpless and disbelieving when they confront change. These emotions may last for minutes, hours,

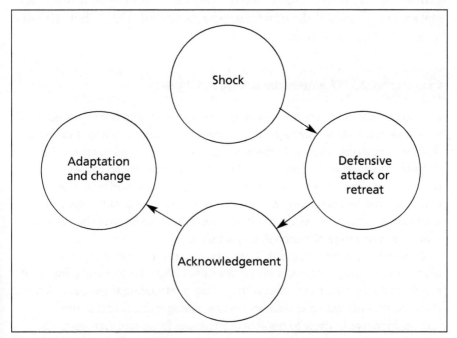

Figure 9.1 *The change cycle*

days or even weeks. This is often followed by a stage when individuals and whole teams may resist the change, e.g. fight against it; argue with their manager, the project manager or colleagues; or retreat by being in denial ('it will never happen') and ignoring the forthcoming changes (e.g. by deleting e-mails and not attending relevant meetings). Again, this stage may last for a short time or even weeks. The next stage is where individuals acknowledge that the change is going to happen and begin to face up to reality. Some people may decide to leave the organisation and find a new job, change career, set up their own business, or retire. The last stage in the change cycle occurs when individuals and teams adapt to the change and incorporate it into their everyday working lives.

Project leaders, managers and workers should be aware of the importance of managing change as many individuals will go through this process for major strategic change projects and operational projects, which have an impact on someone's working life. Some people may work through this cycle in a few days, others take weeks or even months. Within a team, individuals may be at different stages in this cycle, and some people may still be experiencing the after-effects of earlier change processes. Consequently, dealing with change is often a very challenging area of work and a vital area to get right if the project is to be successful. This is demonstrated in the following case studies.

Case study 9.9   Changes to working practices

Richard worked as the contracts manager for e-journals and books in a public library. He had held the same job and worked in the same team for five years. As a result of a restructuring in the local authority that aimed to rationalise different processes and departments, Richard's role was moved to a new procurement department in a different building. He now worked in a team with staff who had previously worked in other sections, e.g. highways and transport, and had a generic job title and description, so he could be asked to procure a wide range of materials and supplies.

Everyone in the local authority knew about the restructuring and re-organisation change process, and had been kept informed by e-mails and open meetings. Richard did not bother with reading or attending them, as he didn't think the changes would affect him. His line manager also said that the restructuring was unlikely to result in any changes to his role. Consequently, when the change process began to be implemented and Richard received a formal letter outlining the changes to his role and with a new contract for him to sign, he was horrified. He went through several weeks of major stress and upset to the extent that he visited his doctor about its adverse effect on his health. He signed the new contract and moved to his new role and department.

After six months Richard resigned and moved to a similar role to his previous one in another authority. Looking back, he said that he wished he had taken more notice of the change process that had taken place and that he had attended the open meetings to find out more about it. He also wished that his line manager had been more engaged in the process and honest with him about the likely impact of the restructuring on him. Finally, he said that the months of stress and anxiety could have been avoided if there had been a better and more engaging communication process, and that someone had sat down with him and honestly let him know about its likely impact on him.

Case study 9.10 The impact of a company merger

Monique had worked for ten years for a small engineering company in Leeds, where she managed the information unit. Monique's manager Jane, the technical director, informed her that the company had been taken over by a much larger one, whose headquarters were in London, and that no one knew what the impact of this change would be on the current managerial and professional support staff in Leeds. They spent some time discussing possibilities and Jane promised to keep Monique informed as soon as there was any news.

After a few weeks of uncertainty, Jane met Monique and told her that the information unit was going to be amalgamated with the one based in the new company, and Monique would have the opportunity to move to London. Following the merger of the two units she would be managed by the information officer currently based in London. She would be able to visit the London office and meet her potential new manager before she decided whether or not to move. The company would pay Monique a generous relocation allowance plus pay enhancement to take into account the difference between Leeds and London salaries.

After visiting the London office, Monique decided to relocate to London and take up the new position; she recognised that it would give her more career opportunities. Overall, Monique was very satisfied with the change to her working life and felt that she had been treated very fairly by the company.

The different strategies required for managing and supporting people through change are summarised in Figure 9.2. As a project manager or team worker it is important to be aware of this process and to take it into account when planning the project communication process or your approach to leading meetings.

Continue communicating the progress of the project Follow up any issues Keep listening Be adaptable Monitor and support team working Acknowledge everyone's efforts	Explain the aim and intended benefits of the project clearly Give the big picture but not too much detail Keep it simple If people are in shock then they are unlikely to remember the details or may misunderstand them Provide lots of different ways for people to find out about the change and discuss it Be available Give reassurance Acknowledge the emotional impact of the change Listen to people's concerns and take them into account – they will help you to improve the project implementation process
ADJUSTMENT	**SHOCK**
ACKNOWLEDGEMENT	**DEFENSIVE RETREAT**
Provide more detailed information Keep listening Support realistic ideas and strategies Involve as many people as possible in the planning process and include individuals who are not in favour of the project Provide direction rather than control Acknowledge people's efforts positively	Allow people to let off steam Give quiet people an opportunity to talk about the changes Listen to them Highlight the positives Be honest about any potential negative impact Keep meetings to the point Don't get into win or lose discussions Use a wide range of strategies Acknowledge the emotional impact of the change Don't take individual responses personally

Figure 9.2 *Strategies to manage and support people through change*

In some situations, the project manager may work through this psychological process herself. For example, you may be asked to manage the closure or move of a library and information service with very little advance notice, or be involved in delivering a major project that is suddenly cancelled when funding is withdrawn. When this type of situation occurs the project manager and team workers experience the change process at the same time as their colleagues. This is an extremely challenging situation as the project manager must provide leadership at the same time as they experience a wide range of emotions. In this situation, it is vital that the project manager has support and guidance, for example from a mentor.

The theme of 'management of change' could easily extend to a whole book. Further reading on the subject is provided by Coleman and Thomas (2017), Hodges (2016), Phillips, Phillips and Weber (2016) and Pugh (2017).

Summary

This chapter explored the people side of projects, considering various themes: managing the project team by ensuring that the project workers are provided with an effective working environment and by developing constructive working practices starting from the first team meeting; working in diverse and virtual teams; working with volunteers, including crowdsourcing projects; and the management of change. The next chapter continues the focus on the people side of projects and considers working in partnership.

References

Coleman, S. and Thomas, B. (2017) *Organisational Change Explained*, Kogan Page.

Hodges, J. (2016) *Managing and Leading People through Organisational Change*, Kogan Page.

Hofstede, G. (1994) *Cultures and Organisations*, HarperCollins.

Phillips, P., Phillips, J. and Weber, E. (2016) *Making Change Work*, Kogan Page.

Pugh, L. (2017) *Change Management in Information Services*, Routledge.

Van Hyning. V. (2016) *How to Use Crowdsourcing to Enrich Your Collections and Grow Relations with the Public*, https://www.cilip.org.uk/blog/how-use-crowdsourcing-enrich-your-collections-grow-relations-public.

CHAPTER 10

Working in partnership

Introduction

Library and information workers have a tradition of networking and collaborative working within the profession and with other professional groups. In the last decade governments, agencies and organisations have raised the profile of partnership working as they see this as one way of meeting the need to develop new approaches to working and deliver services in a complex and rapidly changing environment. There is often a financial driver behind the establishment of collaborative partnership projects. This chapter provides guidance on working in partnership.

Benefits of working in partnership

The benefits of partnership working include having:

- enhanced access to people, resources and organisations
- enhanced ownership, projects that are set up to collaboratively tackle specific problems are owned by partners, so project outcomes are more likely to be accepted and owned by the partner organisations
- enhanced quality, as the involvement of a wide range of people with different professional perspectives can enhance the quality of the project experience and outcomes; individual partners may be more willing to take on new ideas and working practices as a result of the partnership
- increased exposure to new ideas and approaches, as working in multi-professional teams can help partners to broaden their outlook and obtain a broader understanding of their work and their context
- improved use of resources, as partnership working enhances access to resources and leads to more efficient use of resources

- enhanced motivation, as being part of a successful partnership can boost morale and help individuals to develop new enthusiasms for their work, though the opposite may be true too!
- continuous professional development, as working on a collaborative project gives individual workers the opportunity to develop their knowledge and skills.

Partnership working brings learning opportunities for the different partners through 'enforced' reflection on their perspectives and working practices in comparison with those of partners.

Despite the benefits, there are some challenges to working in and leading collaborative teams or partnerships. These may result from long-held rivalries or competition; different values and beliefs; power struggles; differing perceptions and perspectives; the potential commitment of large amounts of time, resources and energy; differences in systems and procedures; differences in organisational cultures; and responses of people or organisations not involved in the partnership.

The process of working in partnership

The process of working in partnership on a project involves an adapted version of the project cycle as outlined in Chapter 2:

- starting the project
- planning the project
- project implementation
- closing the project.

If you are working on a collaborative project with one or more partners it is worth enhancing this process by adding two extra stages: an initiation stage and a reviewing the partnership stage. The initiation stage is where the potential partners, agencies and individuals become aware of the possibility of working in partnership. They come together to start working out whether or not they should work together and explore the potential of the reality of working together in partnership. The reviewing the partnership stage comes at the end: reviewing the process of partnership working, identifying lessons learnt, and considering whether or not there is the possibility of further collaborations. This results in the following process:

- initiating the partnership
- starting the project
- planning the project
- project implementation
- closing the project
- reviewing the partnership.

A summary of each stage of the process for working in partnership on a project is given below.

Initiating the partnership
When initiating the partnership:

- identify potential partners
- hold initial informal discussions
- have an initial meeting to establish partnership:
  – to make introductions
  – to discuss expectations, hopes and fears
  – to discuss how to create the vision
  – to discuss how to build objectives
  – to discuss working practices.

Starting work on the project
The partners will start work on the project and they will:

- Produce a project brief and justification.
- Make a formal decision to go ahead with project.
- Start the project communication process.

Planning the project
When planning the project:

- Work out a project plan.
- Identify risks and potential legal issues.
- Identify a communication process.
- Prepare to document the project.

Project implementation
When implementing the project:

- Carry out the work needed to complete the project.
- Monitor activities and tasks.
- Keep stakeholders informed of project and its progress.

Closing the project
When closing the project:

- Finish off any loose ends.
- Identify follow-up activities.
- Identify lessons learnt.
- Prepare a summary project report.
- Disseminate the project outcomes.
- Close the project.

Reviewing the partnership
When reviewing the partnership

- Consider the benefits and challenges of working in partnership.
- Identify lessons learnt.
- Explore future potential partnership collaborations (if appropriate).

Partnership working is not always a simple or easy process. The following list identifies some of the characteristics of partnerships that fail:

- *Domination of the partnership by one member or organisation* – If one dominant partner takes over this can lead to resentment by other members, who don't feel part of the team and withdraw from the project.
- *Cynical members* – Some partners may be cynical about the project, its funding or working in partnership. This can have a negative effect on the project and team working, and result in a self-fulfilling prophecy.
- *Rotating members* – It is a problem if one or more partners are represented at meetings by different members of staff throughout the life of the project as the project team rarely gets beyond the 'getting to know you' stage and there has to be a constant repetition of previous discussions in order to enable the new members to catch up.
- *Previous history* – Sometimes the past history of the relationships

between partner organisations or individuals can have a detrimental effect on the whole partnership. This is particularly true if members use the current project to sort out old scores and battles.

- *Unequal distribution of work or project responsibilities* – If a small number of people take on the majority of the work this can lead to them feeling resentful that they are doing more than other team members, and other team members begin to lose ownership of the project.
- *Added bureaucracy* – Working in partnership can add another level of bureaucracy to project work as partnership working tends to involve many meetings and careful documentation of events. This can often take up more time and resources than necessary.
- *Inexperienced project manager* – The appointment of a project manager who has little experience of working on projects, working across sectors or working in an intensely political context can sometimes lead to the demise of a project.
- *Political interference* – Political interference into the project, e.g. by senior managers, directors and elected members, can lead to problems for the project manager and team.

Keeping the project together

Once a project is established it is essential that all partners are kept up to date and engage with the project. This is one of the key roles of the project manager who must create and maintain the 'glue' that holds the project together. This glue may be either informal or formal processes, which can be divided into 'soft' or people-centred approaches and 'hard' or procedural and documented approaches (see Table 10.1). Both types

Table 10.1 *Types of project glue*

Hard	Soft
Contracts	Shared goals, values and beliefs
Terms of reference	Common concerns and deeper convictions
Formal project meetings	
Use of project management tools such as Gantt charts	Meetings and networking
	Informal communications including social events
Reporting systems and regimes	
Funding requirements	Informal feedback and praise
Legal requirements	Team culture created by project manager and all team members

of project glue are important. Effective project managers ensure that the glue is in place and spend time on both 'soft' and 'hard' glue. If the project comes across barriers or problems the formal arrangements such as contracts and regular meetings may become vital to sorting out the situation and moving the project forward.

Case studies

In this chapter, I have selected a range of case studies and examples of different types of partnership working to demonstrate the wide range of opportunities and some of the challenges and benefits of working in partnership. These case studies give examples of partnerships between:

- shared services in the UK
- youth services librarians (public library) and school librarians in the USA
- health libraries and occupational therapists in the UK
- a university and public library in the UK
- a university and public library in the USA
- university, local government and business organisations in the USA
- three universities in Australia.

Case study 10.1 Shared services

One common example of working in partnership is through developing shared services where one or more library services identify and share a particular service or set of services. For example, in the UK, many local authorities share their services as a means of saving money and maintaining services, though the change to share services can be accompanied by job losses. Shared services may also provide users with access to services outside their home county or borough.

The concept of shared services is often controversial and a very political issue. Horton and Pronevitz (2014), writing from a US perspective, find the most common forms of consortia or partnership working to be shared digital content, group procurement and delivery; shared ICT platforms; co-operative collection development, digital repositories, interlibrary loans and document delivery; and shared training and staff development.

Anstice (2017) provides a valuable resource on shared services in public libraries in the UK, including news and reports, and more than 28 examples:

merging libraries; a book buying consortium; shared bibliographic services; library management systems, stock and education library services; shared library cards; and shared reading and arts activities.

JISC (2017) announced that JISC will work in partnership with OCLC to deliver part of the UK national digital library. Their partnership will build a new shared service that will aggregate academic bibliographic data at scale, improving library collection management and resource discovery for students and researchers: 'We are working closely with Research Libraries UK (RLUK), the Society of College, National and University Libraries (SCONUL), the British Library, individual representatives from academic libraries, publishers, licensing organisations and service providers to try and really think through how to realise transformational change' (JISC, 2017). This is a very new large-scale project and it will be interesting to follow its progress.

SCONUL (2016) provides a toolkit to support the selection and development of efficient and effective shared services in the higher education library sector. It is in the form of a spreadsheet that identifies characteristics grouped in five areas: strategic, design and plan, operational, sustainability and closure. The supporting documentation provides a useful summary of the development of shared services in this sector.

Case study 10.2 Collaboration in rural Texas, USA

Smith (2014) studied collaboration between youth services librarians, working in public libraries, and school librarians in rural locations in Texas. She found that these librarians engaged in collaborative activities such as summer reading programmes, and keeping up to date with events and activities. Despite sharing common goals, most participants did not participate in the following collaborative activities:

- attending information-sharing meetings
- sharing resources
- sharing information about new resources
- providing homework help
- inviting school librarians to observe and discuss resources and services
- requesting copies of textbooks for library use
- attending school open houses
- setting up curriculum displays
- inviting school librarians to participate in planning sessions
- reviewing materials co-operatively

- registering students for library cards
- offering library event programmes collaboratively.

Suggestions for improving collaborative practices included:

- public librarians sharing information about their programmes and activities with the school librarians
- school librarians sharing information about their programmes and activities with the school librarians
- librarians initiating contact with each other
- librarians establishing mutual interests
- staff being flexible in their availability for meetings particularly as school librarians often have limited flexibility
- nourishing relationships
- arranging meetings and planning sessions.

Smith concludes:

> School librarians and public youth services librarians share common goals, such as ensuring the intellectual freedom of youth, helping youth to develop information literacy skills, and providing access to information. In rural locations, it can be advantageous for school libraries and public librarians to work together to ensure that these common goals are met. While the article indicates that school librarians and public librarians in rural areas in the US have some difficulties collaborating, many of these challenges can be minimized or eliminated by teaching them how to become community partners.   (Smith, 2014, 172)

Case study 10.3 Collaborating to use iPads as a therapeutic resource

Dhanda and Johnson (2017) report on a collaborative project to introduce iPads as a therapeutic resource at Dudley and Walsall Mental Health Partnership NHS Trust Libraries, England. The health librarians worked in collaboration with the Trust's Occupational Therapy Department, which purchased 35 iPads for clinical staff as an interactive tool in therapeutic sessions with patients. Dhanda and Johnson (2017) explain:

> Library Services first became involved with the OT [Occupational Therapy] Department's iPads in May 2015. Due to lack of time, technical expertise, and concerns about tracking the whereabouts of the iPads, the launch of the Therapeutic iPads had been delayed by the OT Department. Library Services,

who had recently introduced their own suite of loanable iPads, offered to collaborate on the project, agreeing to set up and manage the iPads; downloading any applications requested by the department and recording who was responsible for each iPad using the Library Management System – with the proviso that the iPads could become part of the library's collection and both teams would promote the devices as an additional provision to support staff and service users.

The library services organised a focus group with colleagues from the OT Department, which enabled them to understand their needs and possible loan periods, and identify a set of free apps that would be useful for working with patients. A pilot project was established to pilot the iPads.

These were some of the findings from the pilot project:

- Using the apps on the iPad had a positive impact on the wellbeing of patients.
- The iPads helped patients engage with staff and other patients.
- Use of the iPads helped patients with memory loss, e.g. they helped them to remember positive childhood memories. Apps such as Google Maps, YouTube and Google Street View were helpful when talking to patients about where they used to live and work.
- The OT staff found the library staff to be helpful and supportive.
- The iPads saved the OT staff time in identifying, collecting and carrying physical resources.

There were some limitations of the pilot project:

- problems with adverts popping up on the iPads
- the time and expertise used by the library service in maintaining and managing the iPads and apps
- the need to ensure that the apps had been evaluated by OT staff and downloaded to the iPad by the library staff before they can be viewed and tested by the health care staff and their patients.

Following the pilot project, Dhanda and Johnson (2017) made the following recommendations:

- Library Services will look into paying for popular apps on iPads to avoid adverts popping up.
- The library will consider the future of the iPads (given that they have a short life expectancy) and will come up with a plan to replace iPads in the future.

- The library will conduct a case study highlighting the benefits of using iPads as a therapeutic tool.

They also described the benefits of collaborative working as follows:

> Collaborative working made the therapy iPad project a success. Without the library's intervention, the OT Department lacked the technological skills to set up the iPads and download the apps. It would also have been difficult for OT staff to find the time to manage the project alongside their clinical duties. Conversely, without the support from the OT Department, the library would have struggled to identify which apps would be required on the iPads and may not have considered all of the practicalities of patient needs. Furthermore, the library needed the feedback and recommendations from staff who used the iPads with service users in order to improve the service for all staff and put recommendations in place. Working directly with a clinical team also enabled the library to promote the new service amongst staff groups who do not usually use the library, such as Activity Co-Ordinators and Health Care Assistants.
>
> In the future, library staff would like to establish the impact the iPads have had on patient well-being. To make the direct link, a number of case studies would need to be carried out over a prolonged period of time on a one-to-one basis to test the impact on service users. This investigation will form another collaborative project with the OT department.
>
> Library services working in collaboration with the OT Department has shown how valuable partnership working can be amongst departments. The success of the project has encouraged the library to seek out other collaborative endeavours in the future with other clinical and non-clinical departments.
>   (Dhanda and Johnson, 2017)

Case study 10.4 Delivering an online information literacy programme to staff at Bradford Public Libraries: POP-i

POP-i was a collaborative project between Imperial College London and the Library Service of City of Bradford Metropolitan District Council to develop an online learning programme for information literacy aimed at public libraries. The outputs of the project, which was successful, included eight modules on different aspects of information literacy.

O'Beirne (2006) described the project as follows:

The Pop-i project was multi-faceted in its approach: part experimental, in the bringing together of partners from different sectors to focus on a new audience; part instructional design related, in reshaping and extending learning objects; and part technical development, in installing and maintaining a new VLE; and part political, in seeking to force the pace on the digital citizenship agenda. For a project of this nature one of the most difficult aspects of control is to delineate and constrain its scope while at the same time retaining an open mind. There were many interesting and related areas of endeavour into which our project could easily have crept, however agreeing a tightly defined set of aims ultimately ensured clarity of focus.

The team followed the JISC project management guidelines (see https://www.jisc.ac.uk), which were archived in 2016 but still contain valuable information for project managers. Challenges identified in the project included: the need to find an appropriate virtual learning environment; the challenges presented by the selected VLE Moodle owing to lack of technical support within the institutions (although members of the Moodle international community were very helpful); and the amount of data collected, particularly in the project evaluation stage, and its analysis.

O'Beirne (2006) concluded:

At a strategic level the POP-i project delivered a greater understanding to senior managers of the needs on the front-line of a public library service. The benefits of cross-sector working were recognised through the sharing of ideas and the opportunity for personal development through understanding a similar yet different library organisation. The problems encountered by the lack of VLE within the public library turned into opportunities to explore, evaluate, install and ultimately deploy Moodle. This enhanced the personal skills and knowledge of the project team. Both institutions have subsequently installed or migrated to Moodle.

Perhaps the two most positive outcomes of the Pop-i project have been the continued use and development of information literacy training in Bradford Libraries. Moreover the development of Pop-i into a real-life product called Lollipop has provided a way to deliver the benefits of the Bradford experience to many more organisations whether they are public libraries, academic libraries or museums.

Case study 10.5   Utah Accessible Tutorials: creating a collaborative project between a public and academic library

Rogers-Whitehead, Rutledge and Reed (2015) describe their experiences of working in a project as part of the Innovative Librarians Explore, Apply and Discover Utah programme. The project, Utah Accessible Tutorials, aimed to create tutorials to help librarians and information professionals understand accessible technologies and how to use them to support their users. The participants worked in an academic library and a public library. They identified the following challenges of working on this collaborative project:

- time pressures
- availability for meetings
- task ambiguities – it took them some time to identify the project's goal and timeline
- issues relating to the purchasing of common ICT as the two libraries had different policies on procurement and ICT security
- the departure of team members.

The benefits of working on this collaborative project were that team members:

- provided a range of experience and expertise
- had not worked on this type of project so came to it with 'fresh eyes'
- shared a strong sense of shared purpose.

The project was successful and the team members developed three modules and are continuing to work on the content. They identified lessons learnt as follows:

- It is important to have institutional buy-in from senior staff and staff in support functions, e.g. IT and finance.
- Ensure that at least one person from each institution attends each meeting.
- Clarify which ICT tools each team member is able to access.
- Establish a plan with goals and a timeline, and stick to deadlines.
- Create a plan for regular communications and use of tools such as Skype, e-mail, DropBox and face-to-face meetings.
- Share project progress with interested parties, e.g. managers, mentors, colleagues.

The paper concludes: 'Overall, participating in this project was a great experience. We both learned more about other library institutions, their structure, and made relationships in those institutions that will carry on through our careers' (Rogers-Whitehead, Rutledge and Reed, 2015, 82).

Case study 10.6 Establishing campus and community collaboration to host William Shakespeare's first folio at Kansas State University

Hoeve (2016) describes a project in which Kansas State University partnered academic and local government and business organisations to host an exhibition displaying William Shakespeare's first folio. They developed a series of 24 events showcasing the works of Shakespeare and a series of educational lectures for the community. Hoeve describes the project process. It included:

- applying for a grant
- a planning phase (2015–16)
- confirming the schedule, funding, and marketing
- programming
- acquiring the first folio exhibit and materials
- assessing results and outcomes
- discussing whether collaboration would be suitable for future projects.

The project was a success and Hoeve described the lessons learnt from the experience:

- The project provided a blueprint for future collaborative partnerships of this type.
- The project team communicated via e-mail to departmental chairs, library subject specialists and local organisations to explain the project and its scope.
- The grant writing group established a LISTSERV, which enabled them to send updates on announcements, task reminders and meetings.
- Google Docs was used for task management checklists and an events calendar.
- Routine meetings helped to maintain momentum and focus on the project.

Case study 10.7 Collaborative partnership between three Australian universities

Sparks, Saw and Davies (2014) write about a collaborative project involving three Australian universities (Bond University, Griffith University and University of Western Australia), which had very different positions in league tables, funding models and geographic locations. Each university had a converged services model where the library and information technology (IT) operational units reported to a central unit (Information Services or equivalent) and had similar delivery and scope.

The focus for the collaboration was a project on career development that extended earlier work of the Council of Australian Universities Directors of Information Technology in 2010 to include other areas of information management such as librarians, information literacy specialists, e-research professionals and possibly other roles.

Developing the project involved holding a face-to-face meeting between senior leaders from each organisation. Participants at the initial project planning meeting:

- established agreed guidelines for the partner relationship
- defined stakeholder groups
- established principles of trust, creating a shared vision and building cultural awareness.

Guidelines for the collaborative partnership were established that:

- formalised the project lead or manager
- identified potential partner members
- established the frequency, length and format of meetings
- determined the expected project timeframe
- agreed on the chair and organiser of meetings
- established how responsibility was to be shared equally, or alternatively how one partner might take the lead
- clarified how decisions were to be made
- identified the goals of the collaborative project
- agreed the responsibilities, authority and level of resourcing required
- agreed the contractual agreement and terms
- established the governance structure.

This was a successful partnership: the project achieved its goal and was delivered within its timeframe. Sparks, Saw and Davies (2014) stated that the collaborative partnership succeeded for the following reasons:

- The three leaders of the project shared the same business ethics and values of trust, transparency and truth.
- There was a project charter that mapped out the roles, responsibilities and outcomes to be achieved.
- The partners adopted the Chinese approach to doing business, which emphasises trust, empathy and overall balance over the conflicting interests of our group.
- Each partner displayed strong qualities of dependability, trustworthiness and

respect, and they shared a moral obligation to uphold certain standards of business.

These are the collaborative areas that worked well:

- having clear commitment and engagement for the senior leaders
- having a dedicated project manager
- having regular and short teleconference meetings between partners
- sharing institution-specific knowledge and developmental work
- using templates helped standardise approaches and achieve consistency
- holding one face-to-face all-day meeting
- using Dropbox for file sharing
- allocating specific career work streams to each institution.

These are areas for development in future collaborative work:

- involving more people from each of the institutions
- using information-sharing tools such as Google
- agreeing on a series of format templates at the very beginning of the project
- agreeing on a quality standard to ensure consistency and minimise editing work
- considering the effect of potential structural and personnel changes in participating institutions and agreeing a contingency plan to manage such changes at the very beginning
- making better use of collaboration technologies so that participants can use video in some working sessions
- scheduling several half-day review sessions throughout the programme of work.

This is an interesting research paper. The authors use the concept of guanxi and guanxi networks, which originate from the Chinese philosophy of Confucianism, to explain the importance of working collaboratively and emphasising implicit mutual obligations, reciprocity and trust, the foundations of guanxi and guanxi networks. They also use the concepts of 'yin' (collaboration) and 'yan' (competition) to draw out and discuss the balancing acts that took place in the project. They noted that on the macro scale each institution could be regarded as a competitor with its partners, but at project level they considered each other as collaborators rather than competitors.

Summary

Partnership working is a special and increasingly common approach to developing, resourcing and delivering projects in library and information services. This chapter looked at working in partnership, addressing the benefits of working in partnership, and the process of working in partnership and keeping the project together using the concept of 'soft' and 'hard' glue. It contains several case studies to demonstrate the diversity of working in partnership and the benefits and challenges experienced by library and information professionals working on collaborative projects.

References

Anstice, I. (2017) *29 Examples of Public Libraries Working Together*, www.publiclibrariesnews.com/campaigning/efficiencies-2/ efficiencies-sharing-services.

Dhanda, K. and Johnson, E. (2017) *Collaborating to use iPads as a Therapeutic Resource*, https://www.cilip.org.uk/blog/collaborating-use-ipads-therapeutic-resource.

Hoeve, Casey 'D. (2016) Partnering Is Such Sweet Sorrow: establishing campus and community collaboration to host William Shakespeare's First Folio at Kansas State University, *Collaborative Librarianship*, 8 (4), Article 4, http://digitalcommons.du.edu/collaborativelibrarianship/vol8/iss4/4/.

Horton, V. and Pronevitz, G. eds. (2014) *Library Consortia: models for collaboration and sustainability*, American Library Association.

JISC (2017) *New UK-Wide Service Will Transform Library Collaboration*, https://www.jisc.ac.uk/news/new-uk-wide-service-will-transform-library-collaboration-03-feb-2017

O'Beirne, R. (2006) *Delivering an On-line Information Literacy Programme to Staff at Bradford Public Libraries: POP-i – a case study*, www.informationliteracy.org.uk/wp-content/uploads/2010/06/ Public-Library-Case-Study-2006.pdf.

Rogers-Whitehead, C., Rutledge, L. and Reed, J. (2015) Utah Accessible Tutorials: creating a collaborative project between a public and academic library, *Collaborative Librarianship*, 7 (2), Article 5, http://digitalcommons.du.edu/collaborativelibrarianship/vol7/iss2/5

SCONUL (2016) *A Toolkit for Library Collaboration*, https://www.sconul.ac.uk/sites/default/files/documents/1611%20Toolkit_ for_Library_Collaboration.pdf

Smith, D. (2014) Collaboration Between Rural School and Public Youth Services Librarians, *New Library World*, **115** (3/4), 160–74.

Sparks, J-A., Saw, G. and Davies, M. (2014) Mapping the Future: (yin yang) career development collaboration, *Library Management*, **35** (8/9), 629–44.

Index

professional project managers 8–9,
43
professional support 15–6
Programme Evaluation and Review
Technique See PERT
progress reports 99–100
project
aim 53; approval 69, 94;
benefits 107–8; board 32–8,
58–60; brief 68–9; calendar
143; celebration 109;
characteristics 3, 6; closure
107–9; completion 107–9;
definition 53–4; definition of 2;
diary 88; glue 203–4; go-ahead
69; hand-over 107–8;
implementation 97–100;
infrastructure 72–3; initiation
49–53; loose ends 107–8;
mission 4; payments 160–1;
plan 82–5, 91–2; specification
92–3; teams, working practices
177–81; timeline 144; workers
7–8, 175–7; workers, case study
176
project cycle
Agile 38–41; PRINCE2® 32–8;
traditional 24–7
Project Impact 120
project management
group 58–60; history 21–2;
methodologies 3; selecting
approach 41–2; skills 9–10,
22–4; software 140–5, 152–3
project manager 7–8, 11–12
project outcomes 53, 107–8
SMART 74
Projects IN Controlled

environments See
PRINCE2®
Pronevitz, G. 204
protocols 86
public libraries 9, 25–7, 50, 120,
129, 151–2, 170, 176–7,
194–5, 204–5, 205–6, 210
public–private partnership 161
Pugh, L. 4, 197
Pullman, P. 186

qualitative information 118
quality issues 105–6
quantitative information 118
questionnaires 117
quotations 161

recurrent tasks 76
Reed, J. 210
reflection 12–15
Reiss, G. 102
relocation, case study 195
reporting progress 88–9, 101
reports 88–9, 107–8, 122–4, 144–5
research 71–2
resource levelling 144
risk analysis 62–5, 87
risk management 62–5
Rogers, E. M. 56–7
Rogers–Whitehead, C. 210
Rossman, S. W. H. 148–50
Rutledge, L. 210

Saarti, J. 93
Sager, R. 52–3
San Diego State University 150–1
Saw, G. 211–12
schedule 73–81